Raising Creative Teams

Practical Leadership for an Emotional Business

Kevin Frank

Apress®

Raising Creative Teams: Practical Leadership for an Emotional Business

Kevin Frank
San Francisco, CA, USA

ISBN-13 (pbk): 979-8-8688-1245-3 ISBN-13 (electronic): 979-8-8688-1246-0
https://doi.org/10.1007/979-8-8688-1246-0

Copyright © 2025 by Kevin Frank

This work is subject to copyright. All rights are reserved by the Publisher, whether the whole or part of the material is concerned, specifically the rights of translation, reprinting, reuse of illustrations, recitation, broadcasting, reproduction on microfilms or in any other physical way, and transmission or information storage and retrieval, electronic adaptation, computer software, or by similar or dissimilar methodology now known or hereafter developed.

Trademarked names, logos, and images may appear in this book. Rather than use a trademark symbol with every occurrence of a trademarked name, logo, or image we use the names, logos, and images only in an editorial fashion and to the benefit of the trademark owner, with no intention of infringement of the trademark.

The use in this publication of trade names, trademarks, service marks, and similar terms, even if they are not identified as such, is not to be taken as an expression of opinion as to whether or not they are subject to proprietary rights.

While the advice and information in this book are believed to be true and accurate at the date of publication, neither the authors nor the editors nor the publisher can accept any legal responsibility for any errors or omissions that may be made. The publisher makes no warranty, express or implied, with respect to the material contained herein.

    Managing Director, Apress Media LLC: Welmoed Spahr
    Acquisitions Editor: Shivangi Ramachandran
    Desk Editor: James Markham
    Editorial Project Manager: Jessica Vakili

Cover designed by eStudioCalamar

Distributed to the book trade worldwide by Springer Science+Business Media New York, 1 New York Plaza, New York, NY 10004. Phone 1-800-SPRINGER, fax (201) 348-4505, e-mail orders-ny@springer-sbm.com, or visit www.springeronline.com. Apress Media, LLC is a Delaware LLC and the sole member (owner) is Springer Science + Business Media Finance Inc (SSBM Finance Inc). SSBM Finance Inc is a **Delaware** corporation.

For information on translations, please e-mail booktranslations@springernature.com; for reprint, paperback, or audio rights, please e-mail bookpermissions@springernature.com.

Apress titles may be purchased in bulk for academic, corporate, or promotional use. eBook versions and licenses are also available for most titles. For more information, reference our Print and eBook Bulk Sales web page at http://www.apress.com/bulk-sales.

If disposing of this product, please recycle the paper

For my family, who come first

Table of Contents

About the Author vii

Chapter 1 Create Gratitude: Say Thank You (And Mean It)........................1

Chapter 2 Create Transparency: What You Can Expect From This Book......3

Chapter 3 Create Clarity: What Exactly Does A Creative
Leader Do?..15

Chapter 4 Create Foundations: How To Have One-To-Ones 19

Chapter 5 Create Culture: How To Let Your Team Thrive 49

Chapter 6 Create Opportunity: How To Build Your Team.........................79

Chapter 7 Create Creative: How To Give Feedback And Direction 107

Chapter 8 Create Success: How To Sell Work (Or: The Myth Of
The Dog And Pony Show)..143

Chapter 9 Create Gratitude (Part 2): How To Say Thank You 157

Chapter 10 Create Change: Your Creative Vision And Your
Personal Brand 163

Chapter 11 Create Connections: A Little Help From My Friends 183

Chapter 12 Create Understanding: Final Exam 221

Chapter 13 Create Gratitude (Part 3): Thank You..................................223

Acknowledgments 225

Index..227

About the Author

Kevin Frank has been a creative for nearly 30 years, and leading creative teams for the last 15 years. Most recently, he was Executive Creative Director of LinkedIn, where his team was named Advertising Age In-House Agency of the Year and he was named to Campaign's 40 over 40 list. Prior to LinkedIn, he was a Creative Director at Apple and held positions in agencies including the first copywriter at Venables Bell + Partners. His work has been recognized by every major industry awards show, including Cannes Lions, The One Show, D&AD, Communication Arts, and the Effies.

Kevin envisions a creative community where everyone understands that the key to making great work is great leadership. And while Kevin has shared his approach to leading creative teams in articles, posts, podcasts, and on stage, this is his first attempt at writing a book. So please cut him some slack even if it's not quite The Brothers Karamazov. He hopes you like it and find it helpful.

CHAPTER 1

Create Gratitude: Say Thank You (And Mean It)

If you only take one thing away from this book, let it be this:

Say thank you.

I'll have more on the importance of saying thank you later on. But for now, just remember to say thank you. A lot.

Thank you for taking the time to read this book. I hope you find it helpful.

CHAPTER 2

Create Transparency: What You Can Expect From This Book

I believe in transparency. I believe in no surprises (and if you've ever had a boss who unexpectedly taps you on the shoulder and says "got a minute?" you know exactly why). And I believe in leading by example. So I'll start by walking that talk: here's exactly what you'll find inside this book.

I'll kick it all off by explaining why the heck I wrote it in the first place: there are lots of places that will teach you how to be a creative, but no one tells you what to do if you become a successful creative and they put you in charge of other creatives. I'll tell you what a creative leader does (SPOILER ALERT: creative leaders help their teams to be more successful). I'll talk a lot about one-to-ones—why they're so important, how to structure them, what to say, and what a one-to-one is in the first place. I'll explain how to build culture and build a team. I'll give direction on how to give direction. I'll share ideas on how to sell work. I'll help you build your creative vision. I'll ask some friends to pitch in. Neither I nor any of those friends are management consultants, so there will be no charts, graphs, or case studies. Instead, I will share what's worked and what hasn't from my professional experiences, as well as some personal stories. Many of them will be from Apple and LinkedIn because that's where the majority of my

CHAPTER 2   CREATE TRANSPARENCY: WHAT YOU CAN EXPECT FROM THIS BOOK

leadership experience happened, but there will be some from my agency days, and maybe even one from junior high. There will be bad jokes. There was going to be a pop quiz at the end, but since I said I don't like surprises I decided to tell you about it now and call it a final exam.

I write from an advertising industry perspective, because that's the world I come from. But I know there are lots of different kinds of creative teams. There are product designers. There are web designers. There are events, experiential, apparel, game, retail, type, and set designers. There are scriptwriters, photographers, animators, illustrators, directors, publishers, editors, architects, studio musicians, and chefs. There's UI, HI, IA, UX, CX, BX, and PR. And let's not forget all of the other folks who have to work alongside all of those emotional creative types and can't quite figure out what makes us tick. The thing we all have in common is the passion for our work. So even if you're not in advertising, I hope that this book will be helpful.

I'll do my best to walk the talk. I'll say thank you a lot. I will try not to ramble but will occasionally be unsuccessful. On that note, I'll have a thing or two to say on repeating yourself and the importance of overcommunication, which is different from rambling. And to overcommunicate that point, I've learned that no matter how transparent you try to be, people don't always hear you the first time around. So my approach to getting an idea across, whether in a conversation, presentation, or questionable endeavor of a book, is to say the thing I'm going to say, then saying the thing, then saying the thing I just said. So all of that stuff I just said? You can expect to hear it a lot. And one last point on overcommunicating: I'm not only going to repeat myself a lot, I'll do my best to explain why the things I'm repeating are helpful, important, and worth repeating. And while I've been a copywriter for a long time, this is the first book on leadership I've ever written. And in full transparency, it's the first book of any kind I've ever written—I'm better at 60-second scripts than 60,000 word manuscripts. So it will not be as polished as many other books on the subject. I will probably get some stuff wrong. But god help me if there are any typos.

That's what you can expect from this book. That's what you can expect from me as a leader.

A Disclaimer And A Promise

This book is based on my personal experience, and not hard data (that's why I didn't call it *Boring Creative Teams Silly With Scientific Methodologies* or *Raising Creative Teams: An Inscrutable PowerPoint*). The approaches I describe were helpful for me, and I hope they'll be helpful for you. But even if you do every last thing I recommend, you still probably won't be great at them the first several times around.

It's the same as when you started off as a creative. And to kick off my Personal Experience Not Hard Data approach, here's a story about the first ad I ever wrote:

The first ad I ever wrote sucked. It was for a copy test (which was once a thing) to get hired as a junior at J. Walter Thompson (which was also once a thing). The assignment was to write a headline for Trident gum. And here it is in all of its sugarless glory:

"You've tried the rest, now Tri Dent."

Boom!

Obviously, I got better at headlines over the years. But my point is that everybody sucks the first time they try (or Tri) something. So why should you expect to be good at leading the first time you're in charge of a project or a team? Learning to be a leader is exactly the same process as learning to be a copywriter, or art director, or producer, or director, or butcher or baker or candlestick maker. Some people are more naturally skilled than others, but raw talent always needs to be refined.

CHAPTER 2   CREATE TRANSPARENCY: WHAT YOU CAN EXPECT FROM THIS BOOK

Just like you studied and copied other creatives when you started out, you need to study and copy other leaders. You need to be shown what works and what doesn't. You need to learn how to help your team succeed. You need to learn to build relationships. You need to learn to delegate. You need to learn how to give up total control of your creative. You need to learn to stay calm when the client asks for the impossible, or worse, the ridiculous. You need to learn how to give direction and feedback. You need to practice those skills over and over.

And you need to have room to mess up.

Because you will mess up. A lot. And that's totally OK. That's how you learn and get a little better at it next time. Lord knows I messed up a lot along the way before I got any good. And I'm still a long way from great.

So don't lose heart. You'll learn from your failures. And you will fail. You *should* fail. You have permission to fail. Because failure informs success, and I want you to be successful.

I promise that if you keep at it, this book will help you grow into the kind of creative leader you and your team want you to be.

You Can Ignore Most Of This Book

As a cynical Bostonian born of sarcastic New Yorkers who has spent most of his career in California, I used to raise an eyebrow or two at my managers, leaders, and coaches and their touchy-feely west coast approaches to leadership. But even though I've come to believe in the value of their advice, there's still a lot of it that's a bit too artisanally organic for my taste. And that's fine. Because over time, I learned to listen to the spirit and the intention of their words as much as how they were delivered. I learned to pick out the nuggets that I found helpful and develop my own leadership style. I learned to separate the wheat from the chaff, or at least the spelt from the quinoa.

CHAPTER 2   CREATE TRANSPARENCY: WHAT YOU CAN EXPECT FROM THIS BOOK

So, there's going to be a lot in this book that isn't useful for you, or you downright disagree with. My no-nonsense east-coast advice immersed in the healing sounds of crystal bowls may not resonate. You may not like my jokes (you better like my jokes). But listen for the parts that are useful to you. Then incorporate them into your skillset, and adapt them to your own leadership style. Tend your garden of leadership. Nurture it carefully. And as you plant new seeds, behold the miraculous blooming of those delicate flowers as they thrive and reach skyward.

Ick. Please start by ignoring that metaphor.

Why The Heck I Wrote This Book In The First Place

When you first decided to jump into this crazy industry, you were totally focused on learning to be creative. You took classes on how to build a portfolio. You studied award show annuals. You found your heroes, and copied them until you found your voice. You wrote and art directed and designed and coded and shot until your fingers bled. Then you got your big break. You put in your time. You paid your dues. You won some awards. You got to be a successful creative. So successful that they decided to put you in charge of other creatives.

Only nobody taught you how to do that.

This is not a book about how to be creative. There are lots of other books on that topic, written by people who are far better creatives than I am. There are also lots of other books on how to be a Leader, full of fancy charts and graphs and Trademarked Management Approaches™ made by people who are far better at making charts and graphs and Proprietary Approaches than I am.

CHAPTER 2   CREATE TRANSPARENCY: WHAT YOU CAN EXPECT FROM THIS BOOK

This is, however, a book about how to be a creative leader, which is a pretty unique kind of leadership. It's a delicate balance of objectives and emotions. And as far as I can tell, there aren't too many other books out there on the topic. In fact, there's not much knowledge on how to actually manage creative people and teams out there at all.

"Wait a minute Kevin," you might say, "I give my team creative direction all the time."

Ah, but that's not creative leadership. That's creative direction.

Creative direction is telling your teams to make something bluer or greener or bigger or smaller or funnier. Creative leadership is helping them to understand why it's important that the thing should be bluer or greener or bigger or smaller or funnier, and keeping them motivated to make it even bluer or greener, or changing the whole thing to yellow after the 19th round of revisions. Creative direction is a part of leading creative teams, but it's not a substitute for creative leadership.

Now, to be fair, I don't blame the industry for the confusion. Management has not always been central to agency culture, or invited to the party at all. Here's my untested and unproven theory as to why that's the case:

Many agencies are all about making work. And don't get me wrong, creative agencies should be very, very good at making work. That's their main job. So the people who tend to get ahead in agencies are the people who are good at making ads. And that doesn't just mean creatives. Strategists are finding the golden nuggets of insight that makes the work ring true with its audience. Account people are maintaining the client relationships that lead to making the work. Producers are finding the best production partners to make everything look amazing, building schedules, and keeping everything on those schedules. Media people are making sure the work gets in front of the right eyeballs. Creative services managers, project managers, and traffic managers are keeping all of you other slackers in line so anything gets made at all.

CHAPTER 2   CREATE TRANSPARENCY: WHAT YOU CAN EXPECT FROM THIS BOOK

Some of those people are particularly good at making work. They win shiny trophies shaped like vicious jungle beasts or androgynous humanoids or polyhedrons. They bring in shiny new clients, or convince existing clients to spend oodles more with the agency. They work ungodly hours crafting an idea within an inch of its life. They judge awards shows, do thought leadership pieces in trade publications, or even (ahem) write books.

And when the whole point of agencies is to create work, the people who are particularly good at creating work get promoted.

But great agencies know there's more to it.

Just because someone is good at kerning type doesn't mean they know how to manage people. Just because someone can build an airtight schedule doesn't mean they can have a difficult conversation with a direct report. Just because someone can bring in a multimillion-dollar piece of business doesn't mean they can react with calm and empathy in a charged situation. Some people can, but not everyone.

And by the way, the focus on functional expertise over leadership skills (or worse, as a substitute for them) isn't just a problem in creative teams. My wife worked for many years as an attorney at a Very Important Corporate Law firm. And, in the same way agencies are all about making creative, law firms are all about billable hours. Billing those hours in discovery, in depositions, in motions, in court, and writing Very Important Sentences like "in whereto the party of the first part is ipso facto beholden unto the party heretofore referred to as the party of the second part." Bringing in more clients and more delicious billable hours. Law firms (even not Very Important ones) have leaders too. The partners have to manage the junior partners, the junior partners have to manage the associates, and everyone has to manage the paralegals. Now, see if you can guess who gets promoted into those leadership positions. Ding ding ding! It's the people who bill the most hours and bring in the new business, not necessarily the people who are skilled at managing and motivating their teams and their peers.

CHAPTER 2   CREATE TRANSPARENCY: WHAT YOU CAN EXPECT FROM THIS BOOK

One more same story, different profession: A friend of mine is a physician. And by the way, he is not part of a Very Lucrative Plastic Surgery practice—he works in a rough neighborhood. Anyway, one day over coffee he says, "Hey Kevin, you lead a team. Can I talk to you about some problems I'm having with my manager?" (This, by the way, is a dead giveaway that he doesn't work in Silicon Valley. We never have "problems," only "challenges.") He then describes how his manager doesn't give good feedback or clear direction, and doesn't make space for his direct reports to let him know the problems (challenges) they're having with him. The two of them don't have one-to-ones regularly, and when they do they mainly talk about the cases they're working on. I asked how this person got to be in a leadership position, and my friend described how his manager had published some Very Important Research.

Sound familiar?

Now, even though advertising has been compared to brain surgery on more than one occasion, I'm not a doctor. But somehow I don't find it surprising that leaders in the medical field suffer from the same ailment as their counterparts in other industries. And that's the profession that came up with the phrase "bedside manner."

Across all industries, people get promoted to management because they were good at their pre-management level jobs. The academic gets promoted to department chair because they published an important paper or won a Swedish prize. The HVAC person gets promoted to Lead HVAC specialist because she's really good at fixing HVAC systems. The pirate deckhand gets promoted to first mate because he's really good at plundering. And the creative gets promoted to creative director because they're really good at being creative.

So why don't more agencies invest in leadership skills? Well, the key word here is invest. It costs money to train people to be leaders. And not just the hard costs of leadership courses, it's the time spent in those courses when there are perfectly good ads to be made or galleons to be plundered.

CHAPTER 2   CREATE TRANSPARENCY: WHAT YOU CAN EXPECT FROM THIS BOOK

So companies don't invest in leadership skills, employees don't have time for leadership training, and they get rewarded for doing their work and therefore penalized for taking leadership training. It's a vicious cycle.

In addition to time and money, there's one other big thing that gets in the way of people becoming strong leaders:

People who are put in leadership positions may not want to be leaders.

They not only may not want it, they may not like it. And they may not have a natural talent for it like they did for the creative skills that got them there in the first place. So I'm going to give you permission for one more thing:

You don't have to be a creative leader.

Really. It's totally OK to just stay a creative. If that's where your passion lives, you are going to be happier and more successful doing what you love than doing what the industry expects of you. And by the way, that mindset is why you decided to become a creative in the first place instead of suiting up for a cubicle job. Also, if you'd rather be making the work yourself than leading it, your team will know it. Remember, creatives are especially tuned in to the emotions of others. So when you're not happy, they'll be less happy, which means their work won't be as good as it can be, which is going to set you up to fail. And you'll wind up right back where you started.

Am I trying to scare you? A little. But like I said, you can expect me to be transparent. If you're going to take on the work it takes to be a leader (and to read this whole book), I want you to know what you're getting yourself into, the good, the bad, and the Giant Hairy Spider In The Bathroom scary. No surprises.

So, why the heck do we need a book on how to lead creative teams? Because agencies make creative. So they put people in leadership positions with creative skills. But those leaders need leadership skills too. This book is for that.

This book is for you.

CHAPTER 2   CREATE TRANSPARENCY: WHAT YOU CAN EXPECT FROM THIS BOOK

You Know How I Said This Book Was For You? Well, It's Not *Just* For You

This book is also for your team.

One of the big mistakes I made along the way was to treat leadership like it was some kind of secret. I thought that if I let my team in on the management techniques I was using, those techniques would seem less authentic. Or worse, like I was tricking them somehow.

But, as I've already repeated, leadership is about openness and transparency. When I figured that out, I started explaining to my team exactly what leadership tools I was using and why I was using them. As a result, they became more willing partners in the process. It provided a common language for us to use in our conversations and in building our culture. When I threw back the curtain, it helped them to understand that management wasn't a dirty word. I wasn't trying to control them. I was helping them be more successful.

The other reason that this book is for your team is that (gasp!) they may want to be creative leaders themselves someday. And just like those great books on creativity gave them the tools to be better creatives, this book can give them the tools to better prepare them to grow into creative leaders.

So tell your team exactly what you're working on as a leader, and share the tools and techniques you're going to use to lead them. Lend them your copy of this book so you are (ahem) on the same page.

I sure wish someone had told me this stuff way before I became a leader.

How To Eat An Elephant

You can expect to learn a lot of new stuff from this book. And a lot of it may seem uncomfortable, overwhelming, or straight up impossible. Looking out for someone's career is a big job. Managing relationships is a big job.

CHAPTER 2   CREATE TRANSPARENCY: WHAT YOU CAN EXPECT FROM THIS BOOK

Finding talent and building teams is a big job. Giving feedback to creative people who are exponentially more emotional about their work than the average professional is a superhuman job.

Being a leader is a big job. An, exciting, exasperating, confusing, draining, infinitely rewarding big job.

And we're not talking about big like a big creative assignment that's due next week and then you move on to the next one. Being a creative leader means creating change that happens over the course of months, or years. It's a long game.

So one last thing you can expect from this book is that you'll get more out of it if you approach it with this mindset:

Don't try to do it all at once.

Like I said, you're going to fail at some of this stuff. And that's okay. But your likelihood of failure is going to be higher if you try to do too much, or try to skip straight to the expert level. It can get so overwhelming that you find yourself paralyzed and unable to try anything at all. So just try one thing at a time. See if it works. If it does, do more of it. If it doesn't, pull back or stop entirely. When you fail, fail small. As you get more comfortable, you'll find that you can try more and more new things, and your successes will increase.

Here's another way to think about it. I am not an engineer, but I worked in tech for a long time. And the way engineers approach big problems is they start small. First, they build a prototype; they do a bunch of homework and build a piece of hardware or software based on their best guess at what's going to work. Then, they see if it actually *does* work. Usually, some stuff works and other stuff doesn't, so they keep what's good, and go back to the drawing board and iterate on what's not. But eventually, they get to a working model. That's when they scale it up, and produce enough of them until everyone in the world has 24/7 access to cat videos.

You can engineer your own success as a creative leader by taking small steps.

CHAPTER 2   CREATE TRANSPARENCY: WHAT YOU CAN EXPECT FROM THIS BOOK

And by the way, that's the same thing that was true when you first started taking on creative projects—chances are you started with a coupon, a banner, or a copy test for gum, and not a national campaign. But you may have forgotten that because you've gotten so good at creating campaigns. Now we're talking about leading a team, which is a whole new kind of project on a whole new scale.

So, how do you eat an elephant? One bite at a time.

Get your fork and knife ready.

CHAPTER 3

Create Clarity: What Exactly Does A Creative Leader Do?

As a creative, your job was to create stuff. As a creative leader, your job is to help other people who are creating stuff be successful.

Let me repeat: As a creative leader, your job is to help other people be successful.

And, because repetition is such a valuable leadership tool, here it is one more time: As a creative leader, your job is to help other people be successful.

If you've spent your career in a cutthroat environment, I know that sounds counterintuitive. Who are these *other people* you speak of? How will helping them get me that next award-winning campaign for my portfolio?

And just like that, you're focusing on functional skills over leadership skills. See how easy it is to fall back into those bad habits? But focusing on the creative output leaves you trapped in the short term. As a leader you need to think long term, and big picture. You need to focus on your team's development.

CHAPTER 3   CREATE CLARITY: WHAT EXACTLY DOES A CREATIVE LEADER DO?

When you let every single person on your team know that your job is to help them be successful, they work harder for you. They know you have their best interests at heart, and that you've got their back. And when they work harder, it makes your job easier.

Put another way, when you set your people up for success, you're still being creative. Only now you're not creating campaigns. You're creating opportunities for your people to learn and grow. You're creating a place that celebrates their creativity. You're creating safe spaces for you to give them feedback on their growth, and for them to let you know how you're doing as a leader. You're creating a team culture. Sometimes you're creating a vision for your team, and sometimes you're creating a quarterly budget or an employee health insurance plan. But in every case, setting your people up to succeed is an investment in the future. And that's big-picture thinking.

"But Kevin," you say, "I'm a jaded creative type. And that all kind of sets off my BS alarm." I totally get it. I've been known to be jaded and even curmudgeonly myself. And if your passion to keep creating work outweighs your passion for creating a great place for the people who make the work, it's totally cool by me. Like I said, it just means leadership and management may not be for you. One of the myths of the creative industry (and really, every industry) is that you have to be the boss to be happy. But only you can decide what makes you happy. And if you do decide that leadership is the way you want to go, pull up a stool to the Altruism Bar, order up a tall glass of Ego-Free Kool Aid, and put your team's success first. Because your own success depends on it.

Now, I know that success is a broad term—success can mean many different things to different people. Some of your people will want to learn to be better at their craft. They'll want to make creative work that resonates emotionally, sells product, and wins awards. But some will want to work on relationship building skills. Some will want to understand other functions in the department or in the company. Some will want to learn how to be engaging presenters. Some will want to understand your clients' business more deeply. Some might need help picking a health insurance plan. Some will want to have a better work/life balance. And some may even aspire to be managers and leaders. And their goals can change from year to year, or week to week. Sometimes it might feel like they change daily. So, how can any creative leader possibly be expected to know what success looks like for every single person on their team?

Ask them.

CHAPTER 4

Create Foundations: How To Have One-To-Ones

Here's a gross oversimplification of my experience with one-to-ones in agencies. Once a year, I'd have my performance review. (And when I say once a year, that year could be 14 months long.) At that annual-ish review, my boss would sit me down, tell me some things that I was doing well, and some things that I was not doing so well. Those things could have happened at any time over the last 12 (or 14, or 18) months. I could have addressed them long ago, or they could be recent. There was little discussion of how to build on the positive feedback and grow my career, or put together a plan to learn and grow from the negative. To finish off the conversation, my boss would say thank you and give me some more money for the coming year. Or, if the list of things I wasn't doing so well was longer than that other list, my boss would say thank you and not give me some more money. And if that list was significantly longer, my boss might say thank you and show me the door.

Now, while that was (as promised) a gross oversimplification, like all great creative, it's based in the truth and common experience.

You see the problem.

CHAPTER 4   CREATE FOUNDATIONS: HOW TO HAVE ONE-TO-ONES

One-to-ones are the foundation of effective creative leadership. That's why this chapter comes before culture, team building, feedback, selling work, and everything else that's on your leadership docket. I would estimate that I spent at least 50% of my time in one-to-ones. Maybe more. (I could draw you a pie chart showing you exactly how much time I'd spend in an average week in one-to-ones to make the point, but I've been clear about charts and graphs in this book.) And while I may not spend a full 50% of our time together talking about one-to-ones, I promise you're going to hear a whole lot about them.

The Basics: How One-To-Ones Work

So, what exactly is a one-to-one? (If the answer to that seems obvious, great! If not, I won't judge you for not knowing). A one-to-one is regularly scheduled time with your direct reports where you talk about what would make them successful. Think about it this way: if you were working on a creative brief, you'd need regularly scheduled time to dedicate to it. You'd need to do your research. Identify the problems that need solving and the insights that would lead to solutions. You'd need to put aside time to ideate and iterate and revise, until you'd finally cracked it. And then you'd start again on the next assignment. Well, now your permanent assignment as a creative leader is to help the people on your team be successful.

Their success is your brief.

Here's a format for one-to-ones that has worked for me:

First, you need to have them. On a regularly scheduled basis. Ideally every week at the same time.

Every two weeks at an absolute maximum.

Once a year (or 14 months, etc.) is right out.

I know that everyone is busy creating (everyone is *always* busy), and one-to-ones may be a new concept for many folks on your team, so half an hour is plenty. You can always add extra time if you need it. I also try to schedule mine for the beginning of the week. People tend to be less busy on a Monday before they've dived back into their projects. They may have topics for you that they've been thinking about over the weekend that are still fresh. And I find that they themselves are fresher and more open to talking on a Monday or Tuesday than they are on Thursday or Friday when they're worn down from the grind of the week, or their minds are already on the weekend. I also try to be mindful of the time of day—I've found that people tend to be more receptive in the mornings before they've become wrapped up in the work of the day, or find themselves running behind as a result of it. I never schedule one-to-ones at 11:30am because people are hungry. I never schedule them at 1:00pm because people are full. And please, never, ever, ever schedule a one-to-one over lunchtime unless you are actually taking the person to lunch. Because that's just mean. And as a creative leader you can be firm. You can give direction that your team doesn't agree with. You can give them news that they don't want to hear. But you don't ever get to be mean.

Getting regularly scheduled one-to-ones on the calendar is easy. What's hard is making sure that you keep them on the calendar. As we know, everyone is always very busy creating ads and all of the things that go into creating ads—crafting art and copy, writing code, writing briefs, attending client meetings, sweating through endless rounds of revisions, going on lavish productions, stealing ideas from old awards show annuals. But here's another cardinal rule of one-to-ones: that time is sacred. You don't ever get to cancel it.

And here's that repetition thing again: one-to-one time is sacred. You don't ever get to cancel it.

I know you're also busy with client meetings and deadlines and creative reviews (like I said, everyone is always busy). But when you cancel a one-to-one for any of those reasons, any of those *functional* creative reasons, you're acting like a maker. Like a creative. But remember, being a creative was your old job. Your job now is to be a creative *leader*, and

CHAPTER 4   CREATE FOUNDATIONS: HOW TO HAVE ONE-TO-ONES

creative leaders invest their time in their people. You need to prioritize your people over everything. Because that's the long-term play to get to the best creative work.

One point of clarification: you don't ever get to cancel your one-to-ones, but your people do. Part of your job as an empathetic leader is to remember that everyone is always busy creating the next award-winning campaign. Or they have a doctor's appointment that they couldn't move. Or they are chaperoning a school field trip. Or they just don't have the mental energy to show up in front of their boss in a way that feels productive. Hopefully they'll value the time you have together and will prioritize it. And part of the culture you build should be placing the highest value on one-to-one time.

If you find that your folks are cancelling their one-to-ones a lot, that's another issue you can address with them (in one-to-ones!). You may find that they try to cancel more initially, but that's because it's a new behavior you're both learning, and learning new behaviors or changing old ones can be hard. But the bottom line is that you have that regularly scheduled time together, your team members do their very best to keep it, and you are duty-bound to keep it.

Your First One-To-One: Avoiding Awkward Silences

As creatives, we've worked on quite a few scripts. So I figured I'd write a script for your first one-to-one to help you get the ball rolling:

(Open on a small conference room. YOU and DIRECT REPORT are sitting at a table. There is nervous excitement, and a hint of awkwardness in the air.)

YOU: Hi (direct report's name)! Thanks so much for making time to get together. I know you've got a lot going on with (name of Very Important Creative Project), but I hope you'll find our time to be a valuable investment. My job as your leader and manager is to help you be more

CHAPTER 4   CREATE FOUNDATIONS: HOW TO HAVE ONE-TO-ONES

successful at (name of company you work for) and in your career. So we'll spend most of our time together talking about what success looks like for you, and figuring out to help you be more successful. How does that sound?

DIRECT REPORT: Sounds swell, chief!

YOU: Great! One other thing, this is *your* time. So I'll come in with a list of things that I think are important for us to talk about, but I'd also like you to come prepared with anything that's top-of-mind for you. And your list will take priority over mine, unless there's something crucial that I need you to know about right away. Some weeks you'll find you have lots you want to talk about, other weeks we may just spend our time shooting the proverbial breeze. Cool?

DIRECT REPORT: Aces, boss!

YOU: Super! So for our next one-to-one, let's each make a list of at least three things that we see as being important for your success. They can be creative skills you'd like to learn, like getting more experience in interactive or becoming a better headline writer. They can be business skills, like how to be a better presenter, how to manage people, or strategies for managing your time. They can be financial, like how to get a promotion or how to make a bajillion dollars a year. They can be more personal, like how to find a better balance between work and spending time with your family or making time for your physical and mental health. They can be shorter term, longer term, or a mix of both.

Then let's compare lists, and narrow them down to the three or four that we agree are the most important things for your success. Then we'll spend subsequent one-to-ones figuring out how to achieve them together. Does that work for you?

DIRECT REPORT: You betcha, big cheese!

YOU: Oh, and one other thing. Some of these goals will take longer to achieve than others. Some might take months, or even years. But I'm in this for your long-term success. And once we reach each goal, we'll assess where you are in your career path and set new goals for you together. What do you think?

CHAPTER 4   CREATE FOUNDATIONS: HOW TO HAVE ONE-TO-ONES

DIRECT REPORT: Love it, o captain my captain!

YOU: Thanks again for making time to chat. I know one-to-ones are a new thing for you, but I *promise* that if we stick with them you'll be more successful at this company and in your career.

(Fade to black)

As a creative person, you know that we rarely follow the script word-for-word once the camera is rolling. So of course you should say all of this how you would say it and not exactly how I said it (although if you've never led a one-to-one before, it can diffuse the tension to admit that this is your first time, then actually pull out a script and read from it in a very self-aware way). But I will explain why it's important to cover the key points.

First, I start off by saying thank you. Because as a creative leader, I say thank you a lot. And mean it. (And I repeat myself a lot).

Then, I clearly establish my responsibility as a creative leader—to set my team member up for success. Remember, most of your team has never had a one-to-one before, or their experience with one-to-ones is that they only meet with their boss when they're in trouble. Being clear that you are there to help them succeed immediately sets the tone for your relationship. It lets your team member know that you are looking out for them, and have their back. It builds trust.

I also show up with an agenda for the meeting. Everyone's time is valuable, and creatives are often working against insane timelines. Having an agenda sends a clear signal that you respect your direct report's time. Showing up prepared also demonstrates that you value one-to-one time.

Even though I come prepared with an agenda, I make it clear that this is their time. There might be something on their minds that supersedes whatever I think is important that day. As a manager and leader, I'm there for them.

At the end of every request, I ask for my direct report's agreement or permission. This lets them know that this is a collaborative process, and I value their opinion—this is not just me telling them what I think will make them successful. We are partners in their success. For your first conversation, it's 99% likely that your direct report will agree when you ask for their buy-in (because most people want to be successful in their careers). And please don't hold me to that 99% number, as with most statistics in this book, it's not based on real data.

I also set clear expectations and goals for our next one-to-one. This establishes that it will be an ongoing process, and reinforces my team member's role as an active participant in their career success. I'm not just going to show up next time and tell them what to do, we're working together toward common goals. Remember, neither of you has all of the information about what will make your direct report successful. They may have some goals that they'd like to achieve. You will certainly have some goals that you need them to achieve. So you need to both get them out on the table to focus on the most important ones for both of you.

You know how I told you that you should use your own words for the conversation? Well, there's one phrase that I recommend you use verbatim:

I promise.

This is one of the most powerful things you can say as a leader. A promise is a solemn vow. A promise is a sacred oath. A promise is your word. And you are promising to look out for your team member's best interests, and to help them grow and thrive in their career.

Oh, and if you make a promise you darned well better keep it.

Finally, at the end of the conversation, I repeated the same thing I said at the beginning about the whole point of one-to-ones, which is to help my team member be more successful in their job and in their career. Remember how I said repetition is important? Well, repetition is important.

You also may have noticed that I did most of the talking. Since it was the first one-to-one, I was explaining, or overexplaining, how the whole thing worked. But in subsequent one-to-ones, make sure you give your

CHAPTER 4   CREATE FOUNDATIONS: HOW TO HAVE ONE-TO-ONES

people lots of space to talk—at least 50% of the time (not an exact statistic), but really as much as they want. In that spirit, I've taken the liberty of writing this script for how your second one-to-one could go:

Your Second One-To-One: Getting The Cycle Rolling

YOU: Hi (direct report's name)! Thanks for making time to get together. How was your week?

DIRECT REPORT: It had its ups and downs. My daughter made the traveling soccer team! And she won her first game. But scheduling practices around work has been a little challenging.

(YOU and DIRECT REPORT spend a few minutes chatting about personal stuff)

DIRECT REPORT: Also, I know I talked like a character from a 40's noir film last time we met, but this time I'm going to just be myself.

YOU: Oh thank god. That was such a cheap laugh anyway. So, let's pick up where we left off last time. How does that sound?

DIRECT REPORT: Sounds great. I brought my list of goals.

YOU: Me too. Why don't you start? I'm curious to hear more.

DIRECT REPORT: Well, I've been a senior copywriter here for two years now, and I'd like to get promoted to ACD. I'm also in more client meetings these days, so I'd like to improve my presentation skills so I can sell more work. And now that my kid's on that soccer team, I'd like to figure out how to make time for that.

YOU: Those all sound like very reasonable goals. Thank you for putting such a thoughtful list together.

CHAPTER 4   CREATE FOUNDATIONS: HOW TO HAVE ONE-TO-ONES

DIRECT REPORT: Oh, and you know how last time you said a goal could be making a bajillion dollars? Can I have a bajillion dollars?

YOU: No.

DIRECT REPORT: Well, it was worth a shot.

YOU: Yep. Can I share the things on my list?

DIRECT REPORT: Yes, I'm excited to hear them.

YOU: I'm glad you brought up presentation skills. That's also on my list—I've noticed that you don't always come across as confidently in presentations as I think you could. Another thing on my list is for you to gain a deeper understanding of the client's business—you're a skilled copywriter, but increasing your business sense will help you sell more work and contribute to your career growth. One other area that I think is a growth opportunity for you is to learn to write copy for social. You're strong in traditional media, but I think it will help you to be more well-rounded because so much of our clients' work happens online. Do those also sound like areas you'd like to work on?

DIRECT REPORT: Roger that, numero uno! Er, yes.

YOU: And I also heard you when you said you want to be an ACD. I think that's an attainable goal for you. All of those things we just talked about—improving your presentation skills, understanding the business, and having a broader writing skill set will help you get there over time. There will be other skills to learn too, and we can talk about those as we get further along in the process. Oh, and as you know, I'm a parent too, and I totally understand that it can be tricky balancing work with your kids. I'm happy to work together on strategies for that.

DIRECT REPORT: Thanks for saying so, I was actually the most worried about that one. Most of the places I've worked don't want to hear about my personal life.

YOU: Well, you've always got a safe space to talk about it with me.

CHAPTER 4   CREATE FOUNDATIONS: HOW TO HAVE ONE-TO-ONES

(*A pause as YOU and DIRECT REPORT bask in the warm glow of mutual respect*)

YOU: So, for our next one-to-one, let's start to think about ways to work on each of those areas of focus. Then we can brainstorm some specific actions we can take together to keep you moving forward. How does that sound?

DIRECT REPORT: Sounds great.

YOU: Thanks again for making time to chat. I hope you're finding this time as valuable as I do. Have a great week.

I'm not going to dissect this conversation in quite as much detail as I did for the first one, but here are more reasons why I covered those topics:

First, I called it a conversation because it was actually much more of a real conversation. The first one-to-one set the ground rules, but ideally one-to-ones become more familiar and less formal as your relationship with your direct report develops.

I always try to start my one-to-ones on a personal level before I dive into the business of the day. This shows that I care about my team as people, and our relationship is more than purely transactional. It gives us a chance to connect and build rapport. It helps me understand the factors in their lives that could be affecting their work. And more than that, learning about my team's interests, spouses, significant others, kids, and the names of their kids' soccer team and what position they play on that soccer team shows that I give a damn.

This is a two-way street: I share things that are going on in my own life as well, the good stuff and the tough stuff. When I'm open and honest with my team, it shows them that I'm human too (surprise, surprise!) and not just their boss. As a leader, my behavior sets the example—if I share things that are going on in my life outside of work it will encourage my team to do the same. This mutual sharing helps to create a safe space for my team. It builds trust.

"I'm curious" goes a long way. Leaders are curious. More on that later.

The potential goals they bring in and what will help make them more successful are sometimes the same thing. But sometimes they're not. Like making a bajillion dollars. It's your job to make sure all of their goals are aligned with their success.

I ended by recapping what we talked about, which showed that I was listening. And I set expectations for the next one-to-one, which shows that I'm keeping the cycle moving forward.

Oh, and I said thank you at the beginning and at the end. If you noticed that without me calling it out, nice job! You're learning how I think. Thank you for paying such close attention.

Subsequent One-To-Ones: Brainstorming Solutions

Now that you've created a shortlist together of goals to work toward, the next step is actually starting to work toward them. And the way to do that is to brainstorm solutions together.

Luckily, as a creative person, you're already pretty darned good at brainstorming. You know the process—once you get a brief for a campaign, you lock yourself away with your partner and start riffing. You start digging holes. You don't edit at this stage, you can do that later. Create when you're hot, edit when you're cold. You scribble down every last idea that pops into your head. Many of them won't be great, some will be downright stupid, and there will probably be more than one bad pun. But as you work through the problem together, every now and then you say something where the lightbulb flicks on and you're both like Ooooh, that's cool.

And that's one you know you'll dig into.

You can't wait to explore, it, develop it, test its boundaries to see how it works in different media and holds up against the brief. It's the idea that you know is going to keep you awake at night. It's sticky. It's an avenue you know you need to take, because it will lead somewhere beautiful.

And then you do it again to see if you can find another idea that lights you both up.

So treat problem solving in one-to-ones like any other creative brainstorm. Only now you're doing it with your team member instead of your partner. And the assignment isn't how to sell more cereal or deodorant or cloud storage, it's how to solve for the goals you've identified in your previous one-to-ones. Get the ideas on paper, find the ones that speak to you, then refine them and implement them.

Another benefit of the brainstorm approach is that when your team member is part of the problem-solving process, they're more likely to follow through on the solutions. As much as we might deny it, as creatives we know that our favorite ideas are often the ones we came up with ourselves. Those are the ones we're more likely to go deep on and fight to keep alive. When your direct report comes up with a solution to reach a goal, they'll be more excited about putting that plan into action because it was *their* idea.

I'm not going to write another script on how the brainstorming conversation could go—like I said, you're pretty good at that already. But here's what a list of ideas you come up with in a one-to-one brainstorm might look like:

GOAL: Improve presentation skills

AN UNEDITED LIST OF SOMETIMES DUMB BUT MOSTLY HELPFUL IDEAS:

Look for opportunities to present more
Take live presentation workshops
Take online presentation classes
Video myself presenting
Practice presenting in front of a mirror
Practice presenting to my partner
Practice presenting to my dog

CHAPTER 4   CREATE FOUNDATIONS: HOW TO HAVE ONE-TO-ONES

Set ten minutes of every one-to-one aside to practice presenting to my manager

Ask co-workers who I think are good presenters for help and advice

Make a "present present" where I give myself the gift of presenting

Identify people whose presentation style I like and copy them

Learn PowerPoint even though it is my sworn enemy

Try singing my next presentation

Try doing my presentation in different voices

Script out my whole presentation

Wear a "super presenter" costume (with a cape)

Do breathing exercises before I present

Find good book recommendations on presenting and read them

Practice making eye contact. See how long it takes before it gets creepy

Hit myself in the head every time I say 'um' or 'uh'

Use my writing skills to tell better stories in presentations

Use my art direction skills to tell better stories in presentations

Find the dumbest dictionary definition I can to start my next presentation

Practice presenting by making TikToks and other social stories

Ask clients for feedback on my presentation style immediately after meetings

Work on dramatic pauses

Try presenting at different speeds—talk as slow as I can, talk as fast as I can

Picture everyone in their underwear like on that old sitcom

For your next one-to-ones, ask your direct report to narrow down the list to the ideas they're most excited about and think are the most doable. Ask why. Compare notes. Refine. Agree. Implement. Say thank you. Repeat.

CHAPTER 4   CREATE FOUNDATIONS: HOW TO HAVE ONE-TO-ONES

The Virtuous Cycle Of One-To-Ones: A Chart (!)

You know how I said that there won't be any charts and graphs in this book? Well, it turns out that's not *entirely* true. There is about to be one infographic, but it's a very important one. Also, if it's any consolation, it won't be a fancy one. Anyway, here it is:

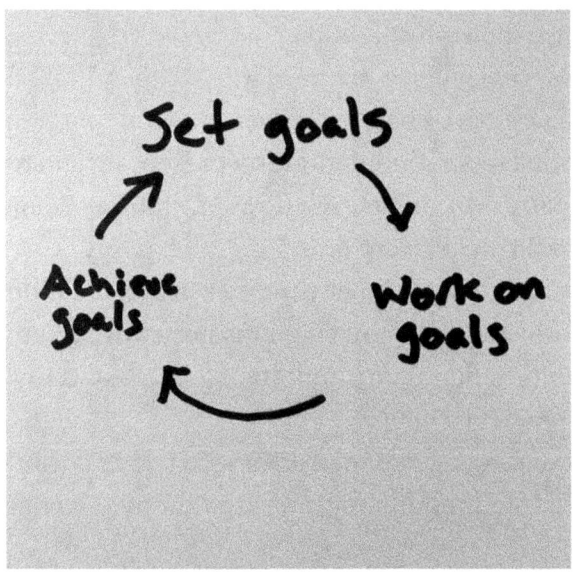

This is the virtuous cycle of one-to-ones (and in case you were wondering, a virtuous cycle is the opposite of a vicious cycle). You set goals, you work on those goals, and as you achieve them you make space to set new ones. And because you've made time in regularly scheduled one-to-ones to talk about those goals and work on them, it makes space for the cycle to perpetuate itself. Each time you achieve a goal, the new goals can become a little harder, building on what your direct reports have learned. You can go deeper, refining the skills they've been working on. Or the goals can become broader, expanding their skill sets into new territory. When you build on those goals with your team, continually pushing the edge of their comfort zone outward, they will be in a state of constant growth. And as you help them grow, you are setting them up to be happier, more fulfilled at work, and more successful.

And that's your main job as a creative leader.

More One-To-One Topics: Going Off Script

As creatives, we know the value of having a tight script. But we also know that often the real magic happens when you go off script, and let the idea take shape organically. So use the one-to-one approach of identifying goals, working on them with your team member until you achieve them, setting new goals, and repeating as your baseline script for one-to-ones. But remember, one-to-ones are their time, and your direct reports might want to talk about aspects of their jobs that may not be directly related to the goals you've chosen. Or they might have entirely other things on their minds besides career growth. So give them space to talk, and give yourself space to listen. You may find you can connect the things they bring up back to career goals you've identified, but you don't have to force it—it's all in the service of helping your team member be more successful, even if it's not always work success. Even when you're at work, you are a human being first and a leader second.

Venting vs. Problem Solving

Sometimes, a team member will come to you in a one-to-one with an issue that's been bugging them. It can run the gamut from An Itch On Their Back In A Spot They Can't Quite Reach all the way up to Who Left The Goddamn Toilet Seat Up Again. It might be about a project, a work relationship, or something that's totally unrelated to their job. Now, they might be looking for a solution. But unless they tell you outright they need an answer, start with this question:

CHAPTER 4   CREATE FOUNDATIONS: HOW TO HAVE ONE-TO-ONES

"Do you want to problem solve, or do you just need to vent?"

And by the way, there's no judgment built into that question. One choice is not any better than the other. As humans, we're wired to want to help. This is called action bias. I'll have more to say on bias later, but what it means in this case is that when someone comes to us with a problem, we want to solve it. But sometimes, people don't want solutions. They just want a safe space to let out their frustration. They want someone to listen. So I'm going to ignore my action-biased instinct to talk about problem solving first, and describe how to let someone vent.

Start by finding the right physical space. Now, this part is important so I'm going to write loudly: THIS SHOULD NOT BE A PUBLIC SPACE. Find an office with a door, and preferably with window shades. Even better if it's on a floor far away from the rest of your team. And then make your team member a solemn promise that you will keep whatever they say in the strictest confidence, unless they pose a danger to themselves or others (did I mention that one of your other jobs as a creative leader is to be a therapist)? And then just let them talk. Or scream. Or throw stuff.

When they're done, and this is another important one, RESIST THE URGE TO PROBLEM SOLVE. This will be hard. So, so hard. I know you just want to help. but that's not what they asked for. So here are your three choices:

1. Say nothing.
2. Say some version of "Wow, that sounds hard."
3. Say "Thank you for sharing that with me. I hope it helped to let it out."

Chances are they'll thank you too.

Problem Solving

If your team member comes to you with a problem they do need your help solving, here's the main thing to remember:

You can't solve their problem for them.

And I know you want to so, so bad. First, because you're a leader. And one of the big myths of leadership is that you're supposed to have all of the answers. Also, because you're a human being. It's in our nature to want to give an answer. We want to help. It's that action bias thing again. But in this case, giving them the answer isn't the thing that's going to be the most helpful. It's giving them space to talk through it with you.

You don't have the answers. But you have the experience to guide people to the answers.

Here's a step-by-step approach you can take to helping someone find their own solution.

Step 1: Repeat the problem back to them (yet another use for repetition as a valuable tool!)

Start by saying, "I'm going to repeat that back to you so I'm sure I understand." Then paraphrase what they said. Then ask, "does that sound right?" If their answer is yes, proceed to step 2. If no, then repeat step 1.

Step 2: Ask lots of questions

Now that you have a general understanding of the situation, it's time to dig into the details. And speaking of general, I'm well aware that "a problem" is a pretty broad thing to be giving you guidance on solving, but as you work hard to create safe spaces for conversations, you can expect to hear just about anything. I am not an investigative journalist, but sticking to the classics is a good place to start: ask who, what, where, why, and how. If the issue is with a project, ask who the client is, what the work has looked like so far, and why certain ideas moved forward while others were left

CHAPTER 4   CREATE FOUNDATIONS: HOW TO HAVE ONE-TO-ONES

behind. If the problem is with a relationship, ask who the other people are, what the relationship history has been, why the tension exists, where the problem happens most frequently, and how things got to this point. Play the questions game. How do you play the questions game? Exactly.

Step 3: Ask more questions

Why would you want to ask more questions? Exactly.

Step 4: Separate facts from opinions

As part of your question asking, it's important to separate the objective facts from the subjective opinions that your team member may have inferred from those facts. Human brains like to know why things happen. When your noodle doesn't have the facts, it gets anxious and makes things up. That way it doesn't have to go pacing around your skull wondering why you haven't returned its texts even though it sent you like 30 messages. This is an especially acute problem for creative people: we're already really good at making things up, so the explanations we invent may be even more elaborate than most. On top of that, creative people are notoriously protective of their ideas, and agency culture skews more cloak and dagger than open book, which makes the abyss of information especially gaping. The result is a lot of creative folks jumping to a lot of unfounded conclusions. Which, by the way, is another reason why overcommunicating is so important.

Your job in this step is to figure out what's a fact, and what your team member's anxious and inventive brain is making up. So here's one more question that's especially useful: "how do you know that's true?"

DIRECT REPORT: Susie Q hates my layout.

YOU: How do you know that's true?

DIRECT REPORT: I sent it to her a week ago and I haven't gotten feedback yet.

Now, it could be true that Susie doesn't like the layout. But, it could also be true that Susie hasn't had time to look at the layout because she's been busy preparing a pitch deck. Or that she's got a sick family member that she's been caring for. Or that she's taking time to make sure she gives thoughtful and thorough feedback. Or she thought your direct report sent her an idea for a layup instead of a layout, and what she actually hates is basketball. The point is, without any real information as to why Susie hasn't responded, your direct report has invented a conclusion. Point this out to your team member, and then send them to have a question-asking and fact-finding one-to-one of their own. And by the way, this is another reason why regular one-to-ones across your team are important; they keep the facts flowing. Eventually you'll arrive at a conversation where you and your direct are just discussing facts:

DIRECT REPORT: Susie Q hates my layout.

YOU: How do you know that's true?

DIRECT REPORT: She told me, and I quote, "Kevin, I hate your layout because it uses too much green." I also have a signed affidavit.

Step 5: Explore possible outcomes

While you can't solve a team member's problem for them, you can help them identify options to move forward based on the facts you've learned from those many, many questions. It's a lot like the brainstorming you do for career goals in your one-to-ones (which was a lot like solving a creative brief). So, here's the next question: "What are some possible ways forward based on the facts?" Coming back to the hypothetical reviled layout, and the fact-finding one-to-one your direct report had with Susie Q as to *why* she hated it so, you might come up with a list of options that includes starting over from scratch, keeping the overall layout but doing a color exploration, having another conversation with Susie about why you chose green and seeing if you can change her mind, or explaining to Susie the difference between a layup and a layout.

Step 6: Choose the best way forward

Now, you'll notice I didn't say the right way forward. Because this is creativity, not math. It's not an exact science. It's not even an exact art. There is no exact right way forward, only the best way forward based on what you know to be true. In any case, it's time for more questions! Because you still don't have the answers.

- What are the possible outcomes of trying that scenario?
- What is the most likely outcome if you try that?
- What is the worst thing that can happen if you try that (and how likely is it that the worst will actually happen)?

So, for example, if you're looking at changing the layout entirely, some possible outcomes might be that you come up with a better layout, that you improve your relationship with Susie because you show her that you're a good collaborator, that the new layout is worse because you didn't have time to think through it, or that you miss your deadline entirely because there's not enough time to do new layouts.

In this scenario, the most likely outcome may be that you come up with something better, and the worst thing is that the client fires you because you miss your deadline entirely. But you also know that you have another two weeks before the assignment is due, which is plenty of time to explore. Or you know that you've only got a day, you've already missed a bunch of deadlines with this client, and they'll go find another agency if you miss this one. In any case, you've finally got enough information to ask one last question:

Based on everything we know, what do you think we should do?

You've empowered your team member to make the decision. You didn't have all of the answers. But you knew how to ask the right questions.

CHAPTER 4   CREATE FOUNDATIONS: HOW TO HAVE ONE-TO-ONES

Easy Conversations

When you've noticed a team member doing something well, take time in your one-to-one to tell them so. And when a coworker or client says nice things to you about someone on your team, don't assume that they're also telling that person. Make sure you pass along that feedback. Tell your team member how proud of them you are, and thank them for making you and the whole team look good. And by the way, don't be afraid to share that positive feedback with your whole team in an email or at a team meeting. Prop your people up with earned praise.

Tough Conversations

Everybody likes to hear good feedback. But sometimes, you'll have to give your team member negative feedback. It might be something you've experienced firsthand or feedback that comes from others. And it could be about relationships, attitude, technical skills, listening skills, or goals they're not reaching. But whatever the feedback is, there's one thing that's true about all tough conversations:

They get tougher the longer you wait to have them.

So have them as soon as you have feedback to share. I know there's never a good time. Your team member is in the middle of a big project. Or they've got a challenge outside of work. Or they're going on vacation next week. Or they just came back from vacation. But the good news is that when you have regular one-to-ones, you already have time on the calendar to have the conversation.

The other good news is there are magic words that make the conversation less tough:

"My job is to help you be more successful. I've had some feedback on you I want to share. It's going to be hard to hear, but we'll work together to address it so you can be more successful."

Then tell them the feedback. Don't sugarcoat it. Don't put it in the middle of a compliment sandwich. Don't editorialize. Stick to the facts in honest, plain, and direct language. Then just listen.

Some people will want to respond right away. In that case, just listen. Others may need time to process the news. In that case, commit to discussing it in your next one-to-one. Then just listen. If they take it badly, just listen. If they take it well, just listen. And when you're done listening, thank them for sharing their honest reaction. Then you can talk.

Repeat that your job is to help them be successful. Tell them you are going to make addressing the feedback one of their goals so they can be more successful. Then address it like you would any other goal. Brainstorm solutions together. Identify the ones that make the most sense. Make a plan to implement them. Depending on the severity of the feedback, you may have to put this goal on an accelerated timeline, and prioritize it over other goals. But when you make tough conversations part of the process, I won't promise they'll be any less tough. But they will be more of a conversation.

One last note of encouragement: I know that tough conversations can be tough on you too. I've had people who were surprised by the feedback, or defensive, or angry, or cried. And that's hard to hear from a teammate you care about. But ultimately, every single person I've had to deliver a hard message to has been thankful to hear it.

And it really has helped them be more successful.

One-To-Many: Checking In With Your Team

The one-to-one format isn't just for one-to-ones. You can use this approach with your entire team. The basics are the same as checking in with an individual, although you may find yourself being more of an MC. But your number one job, and the goal of a one-to-many, is still setting people up for success. Only in this case, it's your whole team instead of an individual.

Like a one-to-one, the first step is actually scheduling a regular team check-in, and explaining to your team the importance of getting together on a regular basis. You don't get to cancel; one-to-ones don't work if they don't happen. I schedule my weekly team meetings every Monday morning. It's a reliable way to kick off the week, and it helps avoid the other business of the week getting in the way. And I come in with an agenda so the team knows their time isn't being wasted, and to let the team know what to expect so they can better participate in the conversation.

My basic flow of a team meeting goes a little something like this: Start by sharing personal stories from the weekend, and find ways to bond over common experiences. I always like to go first, since it breaks the ice. But you may find you don't need to jump in once your team has been working together for a long time and has found their rhythm.

Then, share the things that you've heard over the last week that will be important to the team's success. You have exposure to high-level clients and executives that your team doesn't, and the information you gather from those meetings is vital to their success. Show how your team's actions are already in line with those conversations, and suggest new team goals that align to them. Open the floor to feedback and suggestions on how your team might achieve those goals together.

As you achieve your goals, share them with the team and celebrate them. You can share a campaign that you recently produced. You can share that you won a pitch, or expanded a piece of existing business. You can celebrate an award that the team won. You can share the story of a tough client whom you won over. You can announce promotions and new hires. And whenever possible, let the team that produced the campaign, landed the client, or won the award present their own work. Your job is to give them the spotlight and let them take ownership for how their achievements contributed to the whole team's success.

In each case, have them explain how they achieved those goals, the good stuff and the bad. Don't just share the campaign, share the process of selling the campaign, the ideas that didn't get produced, how they selected the production partners, and challenges with the budget. Share the pitch deck, the thinking behind the pitch deck, which parts resonated with the clients and which parts were met with uncomfortable silences and blank expressions. Share the submissions that won awards, and share the ones that didn't. The idea is that as your team achieves its collective goals, they can learn from each other's experiences and be more successful at reaching future goals.

There's that virtuous cycle again.

Finally, I leave five minutes at the end of the team meeting for open conversation. I'll usually ask an open-ended question like "Is there anything else on anyone's mind they'd like to talk about with the group?" In my experience, the kinds of things people will bring up are typically work-related. But they can also be intensely personal. They can be around team dynamics. Or they can be around current events—it's hard, and sometimes impossible to separate politics, climate change, racial injustice, war, mass shootings, and all of the other difficult things that are happening in the world from work. The point is to be ready for anything, and make consistent time for your team to talk about it. Creating that space helps build a culture of trust, and one of your goals as a creative leader is to build culture (more soon on culture and how to build it).

Oh, and end the meeting by thanking everyone for making time to get together. But you knew that already.

Clients Are People Too: One-To-Ones Aren't Just For Your Team

As everyone in the business knows, the best way to sell work is to do amazing, mind-blowing creative that you just *know* is the coolest thing ever, then get all of your dogs and ponies together in one great big show and dazzle your clients in a 60-minute presentation. Right?

Wrong.

In my experience, the best way to sell work is to build relationships with your clients. To create trust with them. To understand the business problems they are trying to solve—one might even describe these as their business *goals*. And to create a space where your clients feel comfortable giving you honest feedback, and are open to your honest feedback on them. So it probably comes as no surprise that I'm a huge advocate of having regular one-to-ones with your clients as the foundation for those relationships.

You can use exactly the same format as you do with the members of your team: Explain why you believe dedicated one-to-one time is so valuable for their business. Set up regularly scheduled meetings. In those meetings, let your clients know that it's your job to help them be more successful. Identify the goals they are trying to achieve, suggest goals you think would help them be more successful, and agree on three or four to work on as you move forward together. Say thank you.

Success will look different for your clients than it does for your team. They have specific business targets, including dollar figures and market segmentations and success metrics detailed in matrixed spreadsheets. They will probably say ROI a lot. And while that stuff may make your head ache, stay open to it. It's an opportunity for you to learn their language and understand the challenges they face on a daily basis. It's an opportunity for you to grow your own business skills. Maybe even make that a goal for yourself.

Hopefully, they will also have creative goals, and aspire to making award-winning campaigns. But if they don't, remember that you get a say in the goals you're setting together. This is your opportunity to show how creativity and business results are not mutually exclusive. And more than that, creativity can drive business results. You can share your passion for what you do. As a creative leader, you can not only inspire your clients to make better work, you can package it up for them in a format that they can easily digest.

So when it's time for that official presentation, you've already come to a mutual understanding that the idea your team came up with is more than just mind-blowing and cool, it's a common goal. It's a crucial piece of your mutual success. And because you've invested time in identifying and understanding the client's business goals in your one-to-ones, you can bake them into the work. You can share with your clients exactly how the work is solving the problems you identified together, which will make them more successful. And it's all built on the relationship you've developed in your regular one-to-ones.

Managing Up, Down, Sideways, And Diagonally

If your boss isn't having regular one-to-ones with you, insist on it. Explain the value of scheduling check-ins. Suggest using the setting and achieving goals framework you use with your own team. Show them this book. In Official Business Language, making space to let your boss know what you and your team need to be successful is called managing up. But really, it's just a way to build and maintain one of your most important business relationships. Your job as a creative leader is to help everyone on your team be more successful, and that everyone includes you. When your boss helps you succeed, that helps your team succeed. And by the way, your boss wants to succeed too. So the more you have one-to-ones with your boss, the more insight you'll gain into what will help them be more successful. You can find ways to incorporate their goals into your own goals. It's all another virtuous cycle of success, which you can imagine would make a very pretty chart.

Have one-to-ones with your peers. Initiate regularly scheduled time with the heads of account management, production, strategy and media. Use the same basic framework. Ask them what their goals are, and share yours with them. See where there's overlap, and create new mutually beneficial goals that you can reach together.

If your direct reports have direct reports, offer to have one-to-ones with them (if you're in need of more Official Business Language, these are called "skip levels"). These can be less frequent—I tend to do them monthly, quarterly, or on an as-needed basis. When everyone on your team knows they have direct access to leadership, it means they'll have direct access to success.

Have regular one-to-ones with your external partners. Include agencies, production companies, media buyers, and researchers—anyone you work with on a regular basis. It's all an opportunity to understand their businesses and the challenges they're up against, and find ways to solve them together.

I told you one-to-ones would take up like 50% of your time.

CODA: An Unsurprising Annual Review

OK, let's take this thing full circle. Way back at the beginning of the chapter, I described what many of my agency one-to-ones looked like: A once per-year (maybe) meeting with my boss where they let me know the things I had been doing right and doing wrong, some more money or not some more money, and a see-you-next-year to check in again.

So, what if we could go back and re-script those annual reviews into a bigger-picture conversation? Luckily, we can.

Open in a small conference room of an Agency, YOU and DIRECT REPORT are sitting at a table. The mood in the room is relaxed and convivial.

YOU: Hi (direct report's name)! Welcome to your annual review! How are you feeling about it?

DIRECT REPORT: I'm feeling relaxed and convivial. That's because we've built a strong relationship over time, and I know that this conversation is just one in a series of conversations we've been having all

CHAPTER 4   CREATE FOUNDATIONS: HOW TO HAVE ONE-TO-ONES

year. I know exactly what goals we've been working toward, and where we are in our progression for reaching those goals. And because we've been open about everything, both the things I've been doing well and the challenges I've had, I know that there will be no surprises.

YOU: I couldn't have said it better myself. But I'm going to say it anyway because repetition is an important leadership tool. I'm proud of the relationship we've built, and I know that this conversation is just one in a series of conversations we've been having all year. I know exactly what goals we've been working toward, and where we are in our progression for reaching those goals. And because we've been open about everything, both the things you've been doing well and the challenges you've had, there should be no surprises.

(YOU and DIRECT REPORT discuss the goals you've been setting and the progress you've made, brainstorm ideas for how to keep moving toward those goals, and discuss ideas for future goals. You give DIRECT REPORT lots of time to speak.)

YOU: Also, because this is an official annual review, I've written up the things we've discussed today and over the course of the year.

(YOU slide a detailed and well-written summary of the year across the table to DIRECT REPORT, possibly as if you are in a noir film)

YOU: Please have a look over it to make sure it covers everything we've been talking about today and over the course of the year. And let me know if there's anything you'd like to add or discuss more in our next one-to-one. But there should be no surprises.

DIRECT REPORT: Makes sense.

(YOU slide a piece of paper detailing DIRECT REPORT'S new compensation details across the table)

CHAPTER 4   CREATE FOUNDATIONS: HOW TO HAVE ONE-TO-ONES

YOU: Also, here's some more money.

DIRECT REPORT: I hope it's a bajillion dollars!

(SFX: Laughtrack, medium chuckle)

YOU: And even though we've created a safe space to talk about anything, I know that it can still be uncomfortable to talk about finances. So I've detailed everything here so you can review it any time.

DIRECT REPORT: Thank you!

YOU. Thank *you* for your hard work this year. See you next week!

TITLE CARD: *fin*

CHAPTER 5

Create Culture: How To Let Your Team Thrive

Part I. Culture Is The Brief For Your Team

As a creative leader, your job is to help the individuals on your team be more successful. But it's also to help the whole team be more successful. And that's where culture comes in.

So, what is culture anyway? It's the common values you share as a team. It's the set of guiding principles you follow and actions you take together that will help the group be more successful. When you're building your team, you're looking for individuals who have the skills to create the kind of work you envision. When you're building team culture, you're describing how those individuals are going to create that work together.

Culture is the brief for your team.

Culture is the key takeaways you want people to believe about your team, and what you want them to believe about themselves. There's a clear goal. There are guiding insights about your team that inform the culture. There are features of the culture, reasons to believe in it, and clear

CHAPTER 5   CREATE CULTURE: HOW TO LET YOUR TEAM THRIVE

benefits of how it can motivate the team to do their best work. There are mandatories. And like the best briefs, culture isn't created by an individual. It's the result of the common experiences and shared truths of the group.

In companies with a strong culture, you feel its presence everywhere. At Apple, innovation was central to the culture. And it didn't just show up in the products. The way they drew the org chart was innovative. The way they designed the physical space was innovative, from the original Infinite Loop all the way up to the Spaceship. The *pizza* was innovative—some hungry employee noticed that when you took a pizza from the cafeteria to eat at your desk (I said Apple was innovative, I didn't say anything about work/life balance) it got soggy on the way. So they designed a circular pizza-sized container with holes in the lid that let the hot cheesy moist air escape and kept that iCrust crispy. I'm not kidding. They even applied for a patent. It's US20120024859A1, look it up.

As you design your own culture, consider your values and the company's values. Decide on the behaviors you want those values to drive on your team. Build the roadmap for how you'll make sure your team lives and breathes those guiding principles.

Think about how it'll show up as a pizza box.

Embrace The Existing Culture

Unless you're starting your own place and building culture from scratch, you're going to have to work within a culture that already exists. That doesn't mean you can't have your own team culture, but you'll need to embrace the company culture first. Your team culture should reflect the company culture, and if there are differences they should be complementary. And if you want to be successful, and you want your team to be successful (which, as you'll recall, is your main job as a creative leader), you can never fight the company culture.

CHAPTER 5   CREATE CULTURE: HOW TO LET YOUR TEAM THRIVE

I remember the exact Aha! moment when I first understood the culture at Apple. I was a few months in, and having a hard time finding my footing. It was my first Phone launch, and as you might suspect, those are a pretty big deal around the Cupe. The design team was trying to decide on a hero image. Now, when Apple picks a hero image, I don't mean that we were looking at two or three shots that were radically different from one another. We were staring up at a sea of images pinned to the wall. The first was a shot of the phone from the front, and the perspective for each successive image rotated across three dimensions in nearly imperceptible increments until the phone was just a sliver of a product on its side. Then the phone continued its rotational journey until we were looking at its back, a perfect reverse of where we started. Each angle was a mystery to ponder. Was it better to see the full screen and all its thousands of glorious pixels? Or was it more important to show how thin the product was from the side? But if we only showed the side would people know there was a headphone jack on top? If we wanted to show both the screen and the side, what was the right ratio? Did showing too much of the front make the product seem heavy? Did showing too much of the side make it seem too big? Also, if we showed a little more of the back, we could see the logo. For hours, the team discussed and debated the relative merits of each angle. I grew tired of what seemed like endless minutiae, and figured that it was my job as a leader to step in and move the conversation forward:

"Does it really matter? Let's just pick one."

The silence in the room was absolute. People looked at me like I had two heads. Finally, one designer who had been there for several years broke the tension.

"Everything matters."

Aha!

Right then, in that moment, I got it. One of Apple's foundational cultural values was perfection. Dedication to the craft. Getting every

51

CHAPTER 5   CREATE CULTURE: HOW TO LET YOUR TEAM THRIVE

single detail right, because details mattered. That's one of the things that makes Apple products so special, and so innovative. That's the culture that supported the creation of the product, and the marketing. And if I was going to be successful at Apple, I not only needed to understand that culture, I needed to take a good long swig of Apple-flavored Kool-Aid.

That cultural value was so strong that every single person who worked at the company lived it, all the way up the ladder. I was in one meeting with Tim (and when I say that, I don't mean that I was in lots of meetings with Tim and I'm recalling a particular one. I mean I was in exactly one meeting with Tim), and we were showing him a website about supplier responsibility. After reading through the main site copy, he starts reading the legal copy. And then he picks out one little detail and asks a question about it. Think about that. Here's the CEO of one of the biggest companies in the world, with hundreds of legal experts at his disposal, and he's asking a granular question about *legal copy*. That's dedication to the details. That's the power of culture. That's a leader who walks the talk.

So when I had the opportunity to build a new team at Apple, that's where I started. I embraced the existing culture and hired perfectionists who were ready to work every sentence of copy to within an inch of its syntax. But I also wanted my team to be as strong conceptually as they were technically, a skill that was not as culturally valued at that time. So I sought out creatives who applied that same perfectionist ethic to their concepts as they did to their copy. I aligned the skills I wanted on my team to the company's culture to better set them up to succeed.

LinkedIn had a strong culture as well. And while it might seem obvious that it was very different from Apple's, I also discovered that the hard way. At Apple, one of the central cultural values was attention to detail. Apple was not a place where you would Move Fast And Break Things. Obsessing over the details and taking the time to make everything as perfect as it could possibly be was how you became successful. And more than that, it was how you showed your team that you cared.

CHAPTER 5   CREATE CULTURE: HOW TO LET YOUR TEAM THRIVE

When I started at LinkedIn, I wanted to show my team that I cared. So I got very granular very quickly. I pushed pixels with the designers. I trimmed frames with the video editors. And one day, I sat down with a copywriter to look at an email. We tried different ways to construct each sentence for clarity and simplicity, and how different combinations of those sentences in different orders might lead to the most well-crafted version of a paragraph. After about half an hour, the writer stopped dead in her track changes. She stared at me with that same what's-with-the-extra-head look. Finally, she broke the silence.

"Dude, quit micromanaging me."

Aha.

The behavior that was so key to the culture at Apple was interpreted in an entirely different way at LinkedIn. One of LinkedIn's cornerstones of culture was to "act like an owner." Because it was a younger and smaller company than Apple, they didn't have the time to sweat the details to the same extent, and they needed to empower their employees to make decisions to keep things moving forward. So my attention to craft that had been an act of love at Apple was seen as an act of aggression at LinkedIn.

Once I had internalized the culture, I had more freedom to adapt and evolve it to the needs of my team. While attention to detail was received very differently at Apple and LinkedIn, my personal belief is that attention to detail is one of the factors that leads to great creative. Maybe not to quite the same level of Apple, but I know the value of craft and I wanted it to be central to my team culture at LinkedIn. And one of the ways to support craft is through hands-on creative direction. But as I learned, there's a fine line between giving direction and micromanagement. So here's how I worked within the system, rather than fighting it.

LinkedIn also deeply valued collaboration as part of its culture. It's a professional social network, so collaboration and connection were key to professional success and to the company's success. I let my team know that

CHAPTER 5   CREATE CULTURE: HOW TO LET YOUR TEAM THRIVE

my goal was to create an environment that allowed everyone to do great work. And one of the ways we'd do great work was to craft the details. And one way we were going to do *that* was though collaboration. By looking at the behavior I wanted to build through the lens of the company's culture, hands-on creative direction wasn't micromanaging anymore. It was collaboration. At Apple, attention to detail was in the service of perfection. At LinkedIn, I made it in the service of collaboration.

Cut to about a year later. I had worked not only to reinforce team values that would align with LinkedIn's culture, but also to support the creativity my team needed to be successful. We had just launched a brand campaign, and in addition to creating the TV, outdoor, social, and other consumer-facing components, we led an internal-facing effort. One of the assets we created were large canvas posters in our office lobbies around the world. On launch day, I was greeted in the elevator bank by one of these nearly 10-foot high images. The scale was impressive. The photography was crisp and well-produced. The colors popped. But the canvas was sagging just the slightest bit around the edges where it had not been properly secured to the supporting metal frame. I took a deep breath, reminded myself that LinkedIn wasn't Apple (nor should it be), took comfort in how far my team had come in getting all of the other details right, and got on the elevator. When I got off on my floor, one of the art directors who had worked on the campaign was waiting anxiously to greet me.

"Kevin, did you see the lobby posters?"

"I did, they look great. Congratulations and thanks for all the hard work."

"No, did you see how saggy the edges were? We have to get that fixed NOW!"

Aha! That's acting like an owner too.

CHAPTER 5 CREATE CULTURE: HOW TO LET YOUR TEAM THRIVE

I was also able to make an impact on the broader company by embracing its culture. When I joined LinkedIn, part of my remit was to help build the brand; LinkedIn didn't have an awareness problem, but it had an image problem. Like everyone else, marketers had been empowered by the culture to "act like owners," which in this case meant doing what was best for the products they were responsible for. But that didn't necessarily take the overall brand into account, and the siloed approach resulted in marketing that was inconsistent in look, feel, and tone.

As our team worked to create the company's first brand guidelines, we realized it was as much an exercise in culture as it was in design. Some of those marketers in some of those silos didn't want to give up the distinct look and feel they had given their particular corners of the world. They saw conforming to a consistent design system as a challenge to their individual ownership.

To convince them to adopt the new system, I could have recited a long list of reasons why showing up as a consistent brand is good for business. I could have described in painstaking detail the color theory and lighting standards and proportions of the custom typeface and all of the other aspects of a beautiful and well-thought out design system. Or I could have said, "I'm the Executive Creative Director, so this is the creative we're doing." (which might have worked at Apple, but definitely would not work at LinkedIn). Instead, we invited the marketers into the design process. We listened to their business needs and compiled their input. And while it would have been impossible to address every bit of feedback, the important thing was that those marketers who had been so intent on doing their own thing developed a vested interest in the new brand guidelines. They were owners. And the cultural value of acting like an owner had evolved from act like an owner of your line of business to act like an owner of the brand.

To be clear, none of this happened overnight, and it wasn't just my team—we had a lot of help from other internal and external teams. Cultural change is slow, and it took months of stakeholder management at all levels up and down the chain of command to finally win approval. But the shift to build a more consistent brand wouldn't have happened at all if we hadn't approached it from a cultural perspective as much as from a creative one.

Don't Build A Culture Of Creativity

Wait, what? Kevin, didn't you say this book was about leading creative teams?

I did indeed, but hear me out.

Back when I was ranting about Why The Heck I Wrote This Book In The First Place, I posited that people get promoted into leadership and management positions because they are really good at the functional aspects of their roles, and not necessarily because they have leadership or management skills. That, in turn, affects agency culture. When people become leaders because they're good at being creative, they make the culture all about the work. That's what they know best. But in the same way that creative direction isn't creative leadership, the creative work isn't culture. It's the product.

When culture is only centered on the creative output, then it doesn't matter how the creative gets made. People are forced to work long hours. Their ideas are torn off the wall and unceremoniously crapped upon. Backs are stabbed and throats are cut. Chairs are occasionally thrown. People become afraid to share their thoughts, feelings, and opinions. When people are good at making a specific kind of work, they aren't given growth opportunities. They get pigeonholed based on their experience. People live under a looming cloud of doubt, not knowing whether their jobs are in jeopardy as soon as someone who can make better work, or can make the same work cheaper, comes along. Making culture only about the work leads to the toxic environments that some agencies are known for.

I'm not saying don't make creative work central to your team. What I am saying is that creativity is the product. Culture is the environment that supports the creation of the product. Making culture all about the work can still lead to great work, but I believe that a supportive culture will lead to even greater work.

Don't build a culture of creativity. Build a culture that supports creativity.

To get started, here is a long but by no means comprehensive list of values you can incorporate in your culture to support creativity. Use some of them. Use all of them. You have my permission to steal from them liberally.

Part II. A Long But By No Means Comprehensive List Of Cultural Values That Support Creativity

Set People Up For Success

It shouldn't be a surprise that this is first on the list. When you make the culture about everyone being responsible for everyone else's success, it builds an environment that supports creativity. And that's your job as a creative leader.

Relationships Not Rivalries

Rivalry is ingrained in many agency cultures. The account person is the enemy. The other team working on the assignment is the enemy. The other agency in the pitch is the enemy. And, most notoriously, the client is the enemy. While some competition can be healthy, treating your clients and coworkers as enemies doesn't support creativity. Relationships, not rivalries, are how ideas get sold.

That's why I'm such a fierce advocate for one-to-ones. They are the building blocks of those relationships. When account people are people and not just suits, they become valuable allies in supporting creative work. When teams on the same project share ideas instead of holding them close to their chests, it sparks new and better ideas. Clients may care about their business objectives more than they care about creativity, but that's their job. Embrace their challenges instead of demonizing them, then show them how your creativity can solve them. When you invest in the relationship, they trust the creativity you bring to the table because they know you understand and care about their business.

When you support creativity by putting relationships at the center of your culture, the only enemy is being enemies.

Overcommunicate. Overcommunicate. Overcommunicate.

You are in the communication business, so putting overcommunication at the heart of your culture is a natural fit. And I can't overcommunicate enough the importance of overcommunication.

Overcommunicate about the work. When you review work, explain in excruciating detail why you're giving that feedback. When the team understands how you think about creative they're more likely to bring in ideas that are worth pursuing. And when they understand how you think about the business they're more likely to bring in ideas that the client will approve. Tell your whole team about the projects that are going on across the whole agency, and share why they are important to your company and your client's business. Don't just bring the dogs and ponies to a client presentation, describe all of the work that went into putting the show together, why you made the creative and strategic choices you made, and how they support the client's business objectives.

CHAPTER 5   CREATE CULTURE: HOW TO LET YOUR TEAM THRIVE

Overcommunicate about more than the work. Let people know what's going on in your personal life, with your friends and family, and how you are feeling about it all. And not just the happy stuff, no one's life is all rainbows and puppy dogs. When your team knows that there's a real gooey person under that creative leader's hard candy shell, it sets an example that everyone on the team can open up. It builds an environment of trust. And that leads to better creative work.

Since we're on the topic of overcommunication, here's a story from junior high. Mr. Circo was my eighth grade history teacher (and not the answer to any of my Internet security questions). He was a Great Repeater, and one of the things he liked to repeat was "Three times for the human mind." Saying everything three times is how he made sure all those dates, places, and names of obscure battles stuck in our heads. I have no idea whether his assertion is supported by data nor will I provide any, but it's proven to be a valuable piece of advice. When you overcommunicate through repetition, people are more likely to remember what you said.

One notable exception to all of that: don't send a million emails. People freaking hate that.

It's not just helpful to overcommunicate, it can actually be harmful to undercommunicate (or not communicate at all). I am not an evolutionary biologist, but here's the gist of the science behind that statement.

Way back at the dawn of the human species, we hadn't yet figured out which pointy-toothed animals would eat us and which would look totes adorbs in a matching rain hat and jacket. So our ancestors who chose to pet the big doggie or play in the shiny thunderstorm or eat the tasty-looking mushrooms didn't live to pass on their optimistic genes, and those who erred on the side of caution and just stayed home watching 90's reruns eventually became us. It's evolutionarily advantageous to assume things you don't know will hurt you, and that's how our brains are still wired.[1]

---

[1] Campbell, D., et al. A Triune Concept of the Brain and Behaviour: Hincks Memorial Lectures. 1st ed., University of Toronto Press, 1973.

When we undercommunicate, people don't know what we're thinking, and they naturally assume the worst. If you haven't given feedback on a project yet, it's not because the client meeting got pushed. It's because the client hated the work. Or worse, you hated it. And you are almost certainly going to fire the person who did it. In fact, it's looking pretty likely that the client is going to fire the agency. And have you tried looking for a new job in this market? Also, those mushrooms will almost certainly cause vomiting and seizures, and not be delicious in a seasonal salad. Lack of information results in people drawing their own conclusions, and its noxious offspring of rumors and gossip. And that leads to a toxic culture.

So build overcommunication into your culture, particularly if you work at a big company. Tell everyone everything that could be even a little helpful. Repeat yourself so it sticks to the deepest folds of their naturally terrified human brains. Overcommunication leads to understanding, and that leads to better creative.

Be A Mentor

When I was building my team at LinkedIn, I was keen to include talented junior people as well as seasoned creative veterans. This could be a source of anxiety for those veterans. Mentoring wasn't part of the agency culture they came from. Plus, they were busy running multiple projects, and didn't always feel like they had the time to look after less experienced folks. One of my direct reports became so frustrated with the time spent coaching one junior that they ended a complaint by saying, "We're not running a teaching hospital here." My reply:

"Yes we are."

That was their aha moment, and that person grew into one of the most loved leaders on the team. Part of helping people succeed is giving them opportunities to learn. And I had to do more than set the expectation that mentorship was part of our culture, I set the example. I helped that direct report grow. Yes, it takes a significant time investment. But it always pays off. Give a person a fish and they eat for a day. Teach them to fish and they may just create a great campaign for laundry detergent.

Celebrate The Work Behind The Work

There's a difference between making the culture all about the work and making the culture about the work that goes into making the work. You should absolutely celebrate the work you produce. But if you only reward the work that got made, you're building a culture that supports output, and not a culture that supports creativity.

Whenever anyone on my team completed a project, I had them share it with the whole studio. Not just the output, but the entire process that led to the finished product. The strategists explained the thinking and research that led to the insight. The account team shared the meeting strategy and how they addressed the client's concerns to keep the work moving forward. The creative teams shared not just the work that they sold, but the ideas that died along the way. And the dead ideas got as much respect as the ones that moved forward—there are a lot more opportunities to celebrate creativity if you celebrate the dead ideas too. (Fun Fact*: if I took every idea I'd ever worked on, and made a pile of the ideas that got made and a pile of the ideas that died, I'd have one very small pile and one that went to the moon and back a few times.)(*not a provable fact.) When the entire team shares what they learned, it creates a culture where everyone makes better work the next time around.

Champion Work/Life Balance

Hard work is central to many company cultures. But if you make your culture only about hard work, people think they have to work all the time to be successful. A more balanced culture reinforces the value of taking a break from that hard work too.

CHAPTER 5   CREATE CULTURE: HOW TO LET YOUR TEAM THRIVE

There are lots of ways, big and small, to make taking a break part of your culture. One of the easiest is to take a lunch break. This is also one of the most commonly violated breaks—meetings are scheduled over lunch, or people have to use their lunch break to catch up on work that they didn't get to because they were in meetings, or people see other people working over lunch so they feel like they have to work over lunch too. It's one big vicious (not delicious) cycle. One way to make sure that your team has lunch is to have lunch with them. Set aside a few days a week to eat with individuals on your team, and have one day where you get together as a group. This works for coffee too.

There are other small breaks you can encourage. Tell your team to block off time on their calendars for themselves—sometimes they just need time to think, or to not think. Give your team back the time they worked late or over the weekend on that big pitch or crazy deadline. And even though you sometimes have to work long hours, you can work reasonable hours too. Set the example when you do. Wish everyone a loud good night if you're leaving at five. Try like hell not to check or reply to emails once you've left. And if you have to leave earlier than five to get your kid at school or take them to soccer practice, be vocal about that too.

And on the subject of kids, celebrate when people on your team have them. Let the whole team know that you support new parents taking as much leave as they need, and that they'll be welcomed back when their leave is over. And if a team member ever asks to take emergency family leave for any reason at all, let them. Tell them that family always comes first. Reassure them you've got them covered. If they're taking emergency leave, they've got bigger things to worry about than a banner for flamin' hot wings.

You can be a champion for exercise. Look into getting your team gym memberships. I once had a team member who wanted more time to go to the gym, so I put "go to the gym more" in their annual review right alongside the other business and career-oriented goals. I didn't just suggest time away from their desk, I required it.

Take vacation. And I don't mean one week every three years. Use up all of your vacation days, every year. Make sure your team knows when you go on vacation. Check in with them to make sure they're doing the same. When you're on vacation, try not to check your email. And if you must check your email, never, ever respond to it.

Giving your team time and permission to recharge will help them be happier and more productive. And that means they'll be more creative.

Support Extracurricular Creativity

The great thing about creative people is they don't stop being creative when they leave work. Inviting them to share their outside projects with the team supports a culture of creativity by celebrating it everywhere, not just in the work you do for your clients. Make time for it as part of your regular team meetings, or set aside special monthly time to showcase your team's talents. You can even make an event out of it, and have a monthly team lunch where people share what they've been up to (BONUS: this also prevents the team from working through lunch).

I had a designer on my team who was also a street artist. He shared not only his chalk drawings, but how he made his own chalk. I had an art director who was also a children's book author. One CD was the founder of a soft drink company, and had created an entire identity for the brand. An events specialist also ran a coffeeshop, and designed every aspect of the space. There was an ACD whose cat had like a million followers on social media (and looked totes adorbs in a matching rain hat and jacket). I would cue up my band's latest releases, and the team would humor me by telling me how hard we rocked. Sharing our passion for creativity outside of the office inspired us all to be better creatives at work.

CHAPTER 5   CREATE CULTURE: HOW TO LET YOUR TEAM THRIVE

Share The Credit

We've all seen (and, let's be honest, made fun of) awards show credits with multiple slashes. Did all of those people *really* work on that banner? But here's another take on giving credit: In order for that one award-winning banner to live, a lot of other ideas had to die. And a lot of people worked just as hard on those other ideas. And who's to say that the one idea didn't live *because* of all the other ideas that died along the way? There are very few agencies that can get away with bringing just one idea in to a presentation. It was the breadth of the ideas, and the iterations on those ideas along the way, that led to the final winner.

To build a culture where everyone feels vested in the creative, give credit to every individual who worked on a project. The whole team, not just the creatives. And not just for the awards shows. Celebrate everyone who contributed to making all the work, and share it across the team and across your company. Position every project as a team effort.

Embrace the slash.

Be Persistent

Creative people already know how to be persistent. That's how you made it this far. You persist to get your first job. You persist through mental blocks and mediocre ideas to find the creative gold. You persist through rounds of internal reviews to get the idea ready to present to the client. You persist through even more rounds of client changes until the idea is approved. And once the idea is approved, you persist through the same process in production until you bring it to life. Celebrate the persistence it took to overcome obstacles and create something great rather than focusing on how awful the obstacles were. Elevate persistence from an individual trait to a cultural value, and a foundation to create great work.

CHAPTER 5   CREATE CULTURE: HOW TO LET YOUR TEAM THRIVE

Sometimes You Have To Order The Melon

Resources are always an issue, especially if you don't have a huge team. Making sure no one is too important to do every job below them can be a valuable part of your culture. This was one of my cultural cornerstones when I built my team at LinkedIn. Even as we grew, I knew we'd never grow enough to meet the demands of the whole marketing organization. When I started, there was not only a loosely knit creative team, there was also no account services team, no production team, and no creative strategy team. I had to build them from scratch. I needed to hire people who could lead entire departments in the future, but for the moment would be a team of one. I was transparent about this challenge with everyone I interviewed, and I asked how they might approach it. This was how the account person I hired answered the question:

"Well, sometimes you have to write the strategy for the campaign. And sometimes you have to order the melon for the meeting."

That person wound up doing both beautifully. And more importantly, it instilled that cultural value across all of our future hires. It set us up to succeed.

Everything Is An Opportunity

We've all encountered creatives who have done so many multimillion dollar spots that they'd never stoop to doing a banner ad or (gasp) radio. You may not want people like that on your team anyway, but when you celebrate working on any job and not just the big-ticket projects part of your culture, it communicates to the team that there are creative opportunities everywhere.

Another advantage of treating every project as an opportunity is that it creates room for growth. That banner may be a great first creative project for a junior team member who is learning conceptual skills, or it may be

CHAPTER 5   CREATE CULTURE: HOW TO LET YOUR TEAM THRIVE

great first management project for a more senior team member who is learning leadership skills. At Apple, I had an opportunity to lead a team that created buy flows. If you don't know what a buy flow is, it's basically everything that happens after you click "buy" on a website. It's choosing what color, model, shape, and size you want all the way till you hit that all-important "pay" button at the very bottom of the funnel. I didn't find buy flows interesting. No, scratch that. Buy flows were only one yawn away from memorizing names and dates in eighth grade history (sorry, Mr. Circo). But there are people who love buy flows. And as the name implies, buy flows are where customers actually buy the products, so they're pretty much the whole reason marketing exists. And I figured that the experience I gained leading buy flows might come in handy down the road when I wanted to lead multifunctional teams. So I jumped at the opportunity.

And it was the right decision. I didn't just broaden my experience for that future job, I discovered a key part of the culture I wanted to build there.

Be Brutally Honest

Ask someone to name a dishonest profession, and advertising comes in only slightly behind used car sales and politics. And it's not just our long history of making false promises about products that help you lose weight, have more energy, run faster, have smoother hair or shinier skin, smoke healthier cigarettes, schtup longer, or all of the other ways we've bottled snake oil over the decades. We are constantly dishonest with each other. How many pitches or presentations have you been in where the client tells you how much they love your work, but never actually buys it? Or worse, tells you it's perfect but they have "just a few small tweaks." We water down our own negative creative feedback, or don't give it at all. We spin client feedback in ways that won't make our team lose heart. And beyond creative feedback, we are notoriously bad at giving negative performance feedback.

CHAPTER 5   CREATE CULTURE: HOW TO LET YOUR TEAM THRIVE

The good news is that much of the cultural dishonesty comes from a good place. We are scared to hurt each other's feelings. The truth is often difficult to hear, especially when it's about something as personal as someone's creative work. We're being dishonest because we care about each other. But there's a better way to show that you care.

Tell the truth.

Creating a culture where telling the truth is valued supports the creative on every level. It gives you permission to give honest feedback on the work without fear of hurt feelings, and that makes the work better. Honesty in the work about what the product actually does or how it makes you feel improves the work, with no snakes harmed in the making of the creative. And most importantly, it creates an environment where a team can give each other honest feedback on their performance and professional goals, which makes them happier, more productive, and more creative.

Make It OK To Fail

Remember way back at the beginning of the book when I told you that you were going to fail at this leadership stuff the first few times around, and that it was ok? How did that make you feel? Well, your team needs to feel the same way.

By definition, the creative process is trying a lot of different stuff that doesn't work before you find a solution that does. Failure is at the heart of creativity. On top of that, there's no absolute right answer when it comes to creativity, only good answers. That's why people are right when they say creativity isn't rocket science—it's harder. In rocket science, thrust equals $F = \dot{m} * V_e + (p_e - p_0) * A_e$.[2] Always. In our world, two plus two sometimes equals four, but sometimes it equals banana. And when there's no one right answer, it's even more likely to land on one that's wrong.

---

[2] NASA, https://www.grc.nasa.gov/www/k-12/airplane/rockth.html

CHAPTER 5   CREATE CULTURE: HOW TO LET YOUR TEAM THRIVE

To encourage more creativity, some agencies make taking risks central to their cultures. The problem happens when they only reward the risks that succeed and punish the people who take risks and fail. They're given a good chewing out at best, and put on less risky assignments or fired at worst. And that leads to creatives feeling scared. And that leads to less risk-taking and less creativity. And that never leads anywhere good. So, instead of only rewarding risks that succeed, reward the ones that don't. Create a culture where it's ok to fail.

Celebrate the ideas that died alongside the ones that got produced. Pin them up on a memorial wall. Throw a New-Orleans style funeral for them. Seek to understand why they died, so other ideas might live down the road. Publicly praise your team members who created them, and reassure them that failure is part of the creative process. You don't just accept failure, you expect it.

Now, I know that's easy to say in the abstract. If you've got a client that wants big, bold, risky ideas, then go for it. They've already given you room to fail. Also consider yourself lucky, because many clients need to be led by kid-gloved hands to a place where they are comfortable taking risks. Even though you may make room for your team to fail, your clients may not. And part of helping your team succeed is making sure your clients don't leave so they've got jobs to be successful at. But here's the thing: failure comes in different sizes.

Since we've already taken a trip down memory lane to the beginning of the book, remember the part about eating elephants and building prototypes? Just like you can engineer your success as a leader by taking small steps, you can engineer your team's success by failing small. Make one little mustache joke before you go full Skittles. Show the idea as a social post before you pitch it as a Big Game spot. Test the work in one market before it goes global. Try a creative approach for a single project before you change the client's whole brand. Show a more risk-averse client the work you're doing for a more risk-tolerant one, and show them the results it drove. See what works and what doesn't. Share what you learned with the whole team. Over time, small failures lead to bigger successes, which lead to tolerance for taking bigger risks, which lead to bigger successes.

And by the way, feeling safe to fail creatively affects the rest of your team culture. If your team feels like they have a safe space to be wrong, they'll be more likely to give each other honest feedback. They'll feel safe coming to you with challenges they're having in their professional or personal lives. They'll be more honest with you. They'll be happier.

And that makes them more creative.

Be Friends (But Don't Be A Family)

There are very likely data that show the correlation between having friends at work, productivity, and happiness. And you don't need data to know that an environment where your team feels happy and productive is a culture that supports creativity. So create opportunities for your team to hang out together and get to know each other as people, not just as coworkers. Invite them to share what's going on in their lives at team meetings, and invite them to lunches and happy hours. Spend the first five minutes of every meeting or presentation just being chatty. Even though it's not official business, it's time invested in building friendships. Be excited and supportive when you hear about team members getting together outside of work on their own. Hire people who you genuinely like, and you think your team members will like. See if they pass the airport test. (If you're not familiar with it, this is a thought experiment where you imagine that you're on a business trip with this person and your flight is delayed. Would you be happy hanging out with them in the lounge for a few hours?) Foster friendships by making mutual respect and kindness a cultural norm.

But never, ever tell your team that they're a family.

Here's why: your team can genuinely be friends. Long after I've left jobs, I'm still friends with old coworkers. We chat with each other on the phone. We go on vacations together. Our kids go to school together. And some are even still willing to give me the friends and family discount on Apple products. That friendship is real. It's honest. But with the exception of a few married couples, siblings, or media network dynasties, your team is not family. And the moment you say they are, you're being dishonest. And if honesty and trust are traits that you value in your culture, then you need to be honest and trustworthy.

That trust erodes further when you add in the reality of the corporate world. Families don't pay each other to be part of the family. Families don't have shareholders and board members. Families don't leave each other for other families. Families don't lay each other off or manage each other out. Families don't fire each other.

Invest in a culture of friendship. You've already got a family.

Have Fun

It always surprised me how some places that put such a high value on funny creative took themselves way too seriously. You are in the business of creativity, and you got into it because it's fun. And whether or not advertising is as hard as brain surgery or rocket science, I bet it's a whole lot more fun. Some things you probably won't hear around the lab: This cerebral aneurysm is cracking me up! Have you seen Tsiolkovsky's equation? That guy doesn't know his mass from his elbow!

When your team is having fun, they're happier. And when they're happier, they're more productive. So start your meetings with a joke. Slip fun language into briefs. Share a funny story from the weekend. Bond over the ridiculousness of common work experiences. And lean into your own style of humor. You've probably figured out by now that I alternate between dad jokes and bone-dry wit (one of my proudest moments was when a team member told me that he got one of my jokes two weeks after I cracked it). If you're feeling stuck, here are a few classics to break the ice:

How many art directors does it take to change a lightbulb?
Does it have to be a lightbulb?

How many copywriters does it take to change a lightbulb?
I'm not changing a freaking thing.

How many account people does it take to change a lightbulb?
I don't get it.

How many strategists does it take to change a lightbulb?
Why would I want to change a lightbulb?

How many clients does it take to change a lightbulb?
Can we see other lightbulbs?

When you put fun at the center of your culture, it'll show up in the work. But more than that, it'll show up in how the work gets done.

No Expletives Work Here*
*Some Expletives Work Here

Every place I've ever worked (and many more where I haven't worked) has some version of this mantra. And there's good reason for that. It's harder to build a culture that supports creativity if you've got a proverbial bad apple spoiling a bunch of things for everyone. But no matter how hard you try not to hire them, some Expletives always slip through the cracks (pun gleefully intended). The question is how to handle it when they do.

If they're being an Expletive in a way that's illegal or otherwise violates your company's code of conduct, the answer's easy: fire them. But more often, the case is that you've got people who are really good at their jobs,

CHAPTER 5   CREATE CULTURE: HOW TO LET YOUR TEAM THRIVE

but also really good at being jerks. This is an important topic to address in one-to-ones: maybe there's something going on in the Expletive's life that is making them act out at work. Or maybe they know they're being an Expletive, but have no idea how not to be one. Or maybe they have no idea they're being an Expletive and would stop if you told them to.

But culture also plays a big huge part in extinguishing bad behavior. It's much harder to get away with jerky behavior when "no Expletives" is more than just a mantra and you enshrine it in your culture. Expletives in a true no-Expletive culture will either knock it off to fit in, or leave. Win-win.

And how, you might ask, do I know so much about Expletives?

I was one.

When I worked at agencies, I sometimes acted in ways that I wish I hadn't. I didn't take feedback well. I lost my temper when things didn't go my way. I threw the occasional bit of office furniture. I didn't always respect coworkers. It would be easy for me to blame it on my youth or agency cultures that encouraged (or at least turned a blind eye) to that kind of behavior, but blame doesn't get you very far as a leader—even when you're blaming yourself. And because the culture was also all about making great work, I got away with it because I was making great work. But after I left agency life, I had to work to undo the damage to my reputation. As a creative leader, I had to unlearn toxic behaviors and learn healthy ones, both for my own success and the success of my teams.

When I was building my team at LinkedIn, I was surprised when a coworker from my agency days applied for a job reporting directly to me. People have long memories for how you've treated them. In the interview, we spent most of our time catching up on her career, and I learned what motivated her, what she was looking to do next, and why she'd be excited to work at LinkedIn. But then I asked one last question:

"So, I was kind of an Expletive when we worked together. Why do you want to work for me now?"

CHAPTER 5   CREATE CULTURE: HOW TO LET YOUR TEAM THRIVE

After she got over her initial surprise, she smiled, and her formal interview posture softened. By addressing the past rather than pretending it never happened, I demonstrated that I was maybe not as much of an Expletive anymore. It showed the kind of leader I had become, and the kind of culture I was hoping to build. I considered myself lucky when she accepted my job offer. Over time, I regained her lost trust. She grew into a great leader and a champion of our culture, and she helped me to build a healthy environment for the whole team.

Ideas Can Come From Everyone

There may be no single phrase that ruffles creative feathers more than when a client says they have a great idea. Or, since honesty is part of our culture, let's be honest—when anyone but the creative team says they have an idea of any kind. And granted, a lot of bad ideas have led to a lot of creative PTSD. We should have kids acting like adults! We should have adults acting like kids! The headline should say so cool it's hot, so small it's big, or here we grow again! And can we use Snoop? Ideas from outside the team have become such a trigger that most creatives immediately flee the scene with their fingers in their ears singing "la la la, I can't hear you." But sometimes, tucked away in those bad executions is a good idea. And sometimes, the ideas themselves can be pretty good.

And yes, I know the counterargument: we're the experts, why should we listen to Them? They should just let us do our jobs. You wouldn't tell a doctor who says you have a broken arm that your idea was to have an appendectomy. You wouldn't tell a mechanic who says you need a new muffler that you were thinking it would be cool to have the shocks replaced. Yes, they are the experts and you should trust them to make a good decision on your behalf. But to make those good decisions, they had to listen to you talk about your rattly car or excruciating ulna first.

CHAPTER 5   CREATE CULTURE: HOW TO LET YOUR TEAM THRIVE

At LinkedIn, my team had an assignment to promote the now-ubiquitous (and occasionally parodied) "open to work" rings. Saying you had lost your job has historically been taboo, something to be hidden rather than put front and center on your profile picture. Job seekers were scared to admit it, so it was harder for them to find new jobs. So the product was created to normalize asking for help, and take the stigma away from unemployment. It was a great insight with a lot of emotional territory to explore. The client's idea? Let's use an influencer!

My team's knee-jerk reaction was exactly the one you'd expect. Why are we starting with an execution? What does using an influencer have to do with being unemployed? Don't they know we're the experts? Why don't they trust us to do our job? La la la, we can't hear you!

But then we took a deep breath and thought about it. Yes, using an influencer purely based on their number of followers might not have been the right approach (much love for you, Snoop). But maybe there were influencers who fit the brief. People who could give job seekers useful help, advice, and encouragement. People who could reward the brave behavior of saying you were unemployed by opening up their networks.

As you can probably guess, it turned out that there were. The work that came out of that suggestion was some I'm the proudest of. Not just because it won awards, but because it got real people in the real world real jobs. And because it helped our team learn to listen.

Another benefit of learning to listen for ideas is that it helps to build relationships. When people feel like you're listening to their ideas, they'll be more willing to listen to yours. And that's true whether or not you actually use their ideas. When you invite them into the creative process, it will help you sell more work.

Make listening for outside ideas part of your culture. Teach your team to listen to clients when they say they have an idea. And account people. And strategists. And producers. And everyone else who might have a nugget that sparks a creative idea. Yes, your team are the experts in creativity. But part of being an expert is knowing what to listen for.

Tell Stories

Stories are how culture is created and handed down. I can say this even though I am not an anthropologist. And to get meta for a moment, that's also why there are so many stories in this chapter. I could have just as easily made it a page of bullet points (and I'm sure there's a performance marketer out there who can make the case for why bullet points would have been more effective). But you are in the business of storytelling. When you make storytelling part of your day-to-day culture, it manifests itself in how you present the work, how you give feedback on the work, and in the work itself.

Bullet points are for PowerPoint. Stories are for creatives who want to support a culture of creativity.

Walk The Talk

See "Tell Stories."

Be Grateful

I was once on a cereal shoot where we needed to pick out some hero flakes for the flying-through-the-stream-of-milk money shot. The food stylist brought out a tray of wheaty morsels for my partner and me to choose from.

"Which ones would you like?" he asked in anticipation.

"What's the difference?" They all looked pretty much the same to us, but his face lit up as he held up individual flakes.

CHAPTER 5   CREATE CULTURE: HOW TO LET YOUR TEAM THRIVE

"Well, this one is the most friendly and inviting. This one is a bit of a rascal. This one is feeling a little melancholy today. And this one has an unbreakable spirit."

I would say I kid you not, but I know you've had those "only in advertising" moments too. My point is, we all have the most ridiculous jobs ever. Be grateful. Be grateful for your team and the hard work they do. Be grateful when your colleagues support you. Be grateful for a good brief. Be grateful when you sell an idea. Be grateful that the idea had a chance to live at all. Be grateful that you have a job that lets you dream up stupid stuff all day and choose the cereal flake with the sunny disposition.

Say thank you a lot because you are grateful. And mean it.

When you build gratitude into your culture, people feel appreciated. And that lets creativity thrive.

Part III. How To Implement Cultural Values

Easy. Set the example.

Well, easy in theory. A little harder in practice. You have to be diligent about sticking to your cultural values. I might even go so far as to say you have to be religious about it. You need to do more than demonstrate the values you want your team to internalize, you need to embody them. You need to walk the talk. Because the higher up the ladder you climb, the more people look up to you. Just like you will inevitably become your parents, your team will copy your behavior. Like it or not, you are their role model.

If you want to build a culture of honesty, don't just be truthful in the creative work. Tell the truth when you give feedback, when clients ask your opinion, and by sharing what's going on in the company. If you want your team to be resourceful, roll up your sleeves and write some post copy or build a mechanical or order the melon when they need help. If you want

CHAPTER 5   CREATE CULTURE: HOW TO LET YOUR TEAM THRIVE

the team to nerd out on the industry, share examples of new work that inspires you, and the ads you had on your wall when you were just starting out. If you want your team to be cool and level-headed, don't throw chairs. If you don't want Expletives on your team, quit acting like one. If you value work/life balance, make sure your team knows when you're going to lunch, going to take your kid to soccer practice, and going on vacation. If you put overcommunication at the center of your culture, keep a strict schedule of one-to-ones, and repeat a lot of the things you just said in Part II so they stick in your reader's head. If you want to build a culture of gratitude, say thank you. And mean it.

Tell your team, your peers, your bosses, their bosses, and your clients about the culture you are intending to build. Tell them how you intend to act on it. Ask them to praise your behavior when you're living your cultural values, and call you out when you're not sticking to them. Ask everyone for feedback in your one-to-ones.

Also, you know how I said setting an example is harder in practice? The key word there is practice. Leadership takes practice. Setting an example—and all of the other qualities that make a strong leader—are not things that many leaders are naturally good at. They're learned behaviors. That's why you're reading this book. And set a good example you must. You can do the right thing 99 times out of 100 and people will only remember that one time you set the conference room on fire. This is another example of our lizard brains being wired to tune into potential danger. When you behave badly, you are another pointy-toothed creature or poisonous mushroom.

And while we're on the topic, there are few guarantees in life but I can and will say once again with 100% not-backed-by-actual-data certainty that you will mess up along the way. And that's ok, as long as you take responsibility for your actions, apologize, and acknowledge how you'll do better in the future. And then do better in the future.

So keep practicing. Keep walking the talk. Be a leader all of the time, because all eyes are on you. The way to build a culture that supports creativity is to live your values.

CHAPTER 6

Create Opportunity: How To Build Your Team

Here's the most important thing I can tell you about building a team: you are not a creative director. Or an ECD. Or a CCO.

You are the CEO of your team.

And here's the big secret about CEO's: they don't know everything. But the most successful ones know what they're good at, and what they're not so good at. And they hire people who are experts in the stuff they're not so good at to do that stuff. You can do the same. On creative teams, most creative directors come from an art or copy background. So the CD who's a writer may need an expert in art, and vice versa. Creative directors may also be strong in one medium or style—they might be good at TV or print, but weaker in social. They might create great manifestos but fall back into bad puns or mustache jokes when they do comedy. They may be strong on concept but weaker on execution. So they need to hire creatives who can fill those gaps. Many creative leaders also have other departments under them, so they need experts in production, strategy, account service, media, PR, and operations who can help them make better decisions.

Being a CEO means delegating. This is one of the hardest leadership skills to learn after you've spent your career nudging every pixel into place, finding just the right word, or otherwise honing your craft. But now you need to have time not only to oversee all of the people pushing those pixels and smithing those words, but to build the processes and systems that make the space for them to be creative. You need to give up the degree of control you're used to having over the work. And it's not just delegating functional creative skills. While this book will help you grow your leadership skills, there will always be people who are better managers, presenters, and relationship builders than you. Resist the urge to feel threatened by them. Instead, hire them. Give them ownership of their specialties, and let them be the resident experts. Lean on them for advice. Learn from them so you grow your own expertise and keep growing as a leader. Like I said, it's hard. But it's easier when you surround yourself with people you trust.

Create The Organizational System

Part of being a CEO is building a structure for your team so you can surround yourself with those aforementioned trustworthy folks. You need to create the system. This is especially true if you're building an agency or a team from the ground up. But even if you're leading an existing team, a scalable model helps you plan for the future when your team may need to expand in new directions or you need to augment existing capabilities. What does the perfect combination of skills, experience, team size, and projects actually look like? The answer, like so many others when you're a leader, is that it depends. Just like there's no one culture that's right for every team, there's no one organizational system that's right for every team. There's only the one that's right for your team.

The teams I created at Apple and LinkedIn were very different. Apple was a company of specialists because to achieve the level of detail the culture demanded, they needed people who were expert in each facet of each project. Also because they could afford to be. There were over 1,000 people on the marcom team when I left, which meant a lot of people with

CHAPTER 6   CREATE OPPORTUNITY: HOW TO BUILD YOUR TEAM

very specific skills filling a lot of niches. And because my background was as a copywriter, I led specialized teams of writers. My largest team of writers worked on the even more specialized area of interactive campaigns. Only here's the thing: I had relatively little interactive experience. But I did have a lot of management and creative experience, So I approached the problem not just as a CD, but as the CEO of my team, and built a system within the system.

I had 12 slots to work with, so I organized them into three teams of four writers each; three ACDs leading a team of a senior, midlevel, and junior writer. The system that I built within that tidy little org chart focused on three core interactive strengths, one for each team. One team was more broadly conceptual, and had the expertise to tell engaging stories online. One was focused on the craft of writing, since we were often creating sites that were several pages deep. And one was more technical, and knew the capabilities of the web in ways that were outside of my expertise.

And while each team was focused on its specialty, the lines of communication were always open between them, and me. In addition to working on projects together, I made sure the ACD's had regular one-to-ones with each other. That way, they could problem solve together, and share their specialized skills with each other. And in turn, they passed that knowledge on to their teams. And they also passed that knowledge on to me. The result was a team structure that worked within Apple's culture of specialists, and a team environment that created room for everyone to grow.

At LinkedIn I was essentially building the team from scratch. I had a few more staff to work with than I did at Apple, but not as many as I wanted. I had about 15 (although that number thankfully got bigger as the team became more successful). Now, you can still do a lot with 15 people. But part of my remit was to lead creative across all of LinkedIn's lines of business, which included consumer as well as B2B—recruiting, sales, marketing, and learning. And that marketing happened across all media channels. It was like having an agency with five multimillion

CHAPTER 6   CREATE OPPORTUNITY: HOW TO BUILD YOUR TEAM

dollar accounts and a handful of people to run them. And did I mention there were a million marketers with a gajillion projects for our handful of people? And did I also mention that at the time I joined the company, my team's relationships with the marketers were neutral or non-existent at best, and Red Sox/Yankees at worst? The approach I used at Apple was not going to be a good fit for the team I was creating at LinkedIn.

I needed to design a system that allowed us to do all of the work that was being asked of us, build relationships, and had the ability to scale as those relationships deepened and our scope grew. We landed on a three-pronged model that kept us connected to our clients in a way that best suited each: If we could take on a project ourselves, we would. When we couldn't do the work ourselves (or if a client wasn't ready to trust us yet), we'd help our clients find good agency partners, and help manage those partners since we spoke Advertising. Finally, we'd have regular office hours where clients could come to us with questions or bounce creative ideas off of us. The positions I created within the system were based on an agency model of creative, account, production, and strategy, but since we needed to manage external agencies, those roles would be a hybrid of leading internal and external teams.

Then I had to find people who were talented enough to succeed in that model, and crazy enough to come along for the ride. I didn't have the resources to hire a team of specialists. But I wanted to build a team with high creative standards, so I still needed people who were experts in their disciplines. I needed to hire people who could be both specialists and generalists. I needed people who could manage client relationships and agency relationships. I needed creatives who could think strategically. I needed producers who could think creatively. I needed account people who knew that sometimes you had to order the melon. That's where culture came in—I looked for leaders who were willing to do not only their jobs but every job below them. And I was brutally honest with those leaders that they might be a department of one at the outset. Think about that for a minute, a single person running a multimillion dollar piece of

CHAPTER 6   CREATE OPPORTUNITY: HOW TO BUILD YOUR TEAM

business at an agency. Like I said, I needed some crazy people. And during the interview process, I told my future team that it was my job to set them up to succeed, but it was ok for them to fail along the way—given the challenges we were up against, I fully expected that there would be failures.

And let's not forget that I wasn't the best at every single one of those jobs myself. I was the CEO of my team, so I needed to be aware of my own strengths and weaknesses. After years in the business, I knew a lot about writing, and I knew enough about art direction, design, production, and account management to lead those teams. But I am an introvert. And like many creatives, I can be outspoken. And as you're well aware by now, I still have a bit of a sarcastic streak (though I'm not an Expletive anymore). That's not to say I can't put on my charming hat in client meetings, it's just not a hat that goes with my strongest suit. So as important as every function was to my team, I knew I needed a head of account service who was great at (and loved) to build relationships, run client meetings, and shake all the hands and kiss all the babies that I didn't like shaking or kissing. I'd also been sequestered from the advertising world inside of Apple's full-service in-house agency for nearly eight years, and had fallen out of touch with the production community. So I needed a head of production that not only had a finger on the pulse of the discipline, but was wired to the very heart of it. And even though I knew enough about art direction and design to lead art directors and designers, I am not an art director or designer. So I needed leaders who were, and who could help me make better decisions about design and art direction.

At first, we scrounged for every project. But over the years my team built relationships and trust with our business partners, and we had more opportunities than we could handle. So many, in fact, that we had to build other systems. One for staffing that allowed us to borrow headcount from internal clients to work on their projects exclusively, or have them hire creatives onto their teams that we could manage as part of ours. And another system for deciding which projects we'd take on, based on company priorities, priorities for each line of business, and my own team's creative priorities. Luckily I had also hired someone who was much better at making matrixed spreadsheets than I was.

How did I know that it was the right model? I didn't. What I did know would work were my principles. Do my homework on the needs of the company and our internal clients. Hire people that complemented my strengths and compensated for my weaknesses. Put their success at the center of my responsibility as their leader. I had to adjust along the way as the business evolved and my team evolved with it. I built prototypes of my organization, iterated on them, and scaled them when I had a working model. Mistakes were made. I made mistakes. It wasn't an exact science.

But neither is creativity.

What system is going to work for you? It depends. It depends. It depends. But start with these questions. What are the business and creative problems you need to solve? What kinds of clients will you be working with? What kinds of projects will you be working on? What's the company culture? What's your budget? How many people do you have? What are their strengths and weaknesses? What are your strengths and weaknesses? Who can you hire or lean on to help? Then make informed decisions. Engineer your organization. Build a prototype. Iterate on what's working and what's not. Scale it up when you're ready.

You can build a traditional agency model, where art directors and writers partner up to create the campaign idea, and the other creatives on the team help them to execute. You can bring in those other creatives as part of the core team. You can build a team within a single discipline of designers, writers, artists, or interactive experts. You can build a start-to-finish model where your team handles everything from conception through production. And by the way, production doesn't have to be multimillion dollar boondoggles. The rise of makers, content creators, and other writer/director/editor creatives who can do it all from that little black rectangle in their pockets can help you churn out a lot of ideas quickly. You can allocate your budget to a smaller team of more senior people, or

CHAPTER 6   CREATE OPPORTUNITY: HOW TO BUILD YOUR TEAM

a larger team of more junior people. If you're the AOR for most of your clients, you can invest in more full-time employees. If you do mostly project work, you can rely on an experienced core team and build a deep bench of freelancers.

You can organize your team by client or by product or by medium. Going deep in specific areas is also a useful model if you need to build expertise, or build relationships. You can have everyone work on everything if you're short on headcount, though that might also suggest you're taking on too much work too quickly. Rotating people through clients on a tour-of-duty after six months or a year can keep your team fresh and engaged. Or you can keep the senior people on a single client and shuffle your more junior teams from time to time.

If you work brand-side, you can build a model where you create all of the work yourself. Or you can only take on certain kinds of projects, and let external agencies handle the rest. Or you can let external agencies handle everything and hire senior people to supervise them. You can also embed your teams in external agencies if you have the resources, or have external agencies send in reinforcements to work side-by-side your team if you're understaffed. If you have clients who advertise on your platform, you can build a team who advise their agencies on the kinds of creative that work best in those spaces. And if you work agency-side for a client with an in-house creative team, you can build the mirror image of those systems.

If you work for an international company, you can build a centralized model where all the work is created in one office and localized by creatives in each country or region. This is useful when your company, client, or culture needs absolute consistency, like a certain fruit company I worked for. Or you can build a decentralized system where the concept is created in one location but each creative team has the freedom to interpret and adapt the idea to the needs of their markets, like a certain professional networking site I worked for.

And the thing that all of these models have in common is that you don't have to create them all by yourself. You can ask your peers at other

CHAPTER 6   CREATE OPPORTUNITY: HOW TO BUILD YOUR TEAM

companies or within your own what they've tried and what they've learned. Just like you look to other creative leaders for inspiration, you can look to other leaders, creative or otherwise, for organizational inspiration. Copy some or all of the parts of their organizations that make sense for you. If you have the resources, you can hire someone who has experience designing teams. Even if building organizational models is one of those things you're not so good at, you can lean on other people who complement your core creative strengths.

You are the CEO of your team.

Other Obligatory Metaphors

A confession: I don't watch a lot of sports. But if I did, this is the part in most leadership books where I would be required to say that you are the quarterback who's coordinating the plays and leading the team down the field to victory. Or you're the team manager who turns your ragtag bunch of misfits around and goes on to win the league championship. Wait, maybe you're the towel boy that's the glue that holds the team together?

Let's try music, since that's a little closer to my heart. You are the conductor of your orchestra. You don't need to play every instrument, but you need to have a deep understanding of what kind of music you intend to play, and what that music will sound like. You need to know how to give your first violinist room to shine but not leave the brass playing sad trombones. You need to have a variety and balance of musicians, because no one wants to hear an orchestra of glockenspiels (except Leopold Müller of Feuchtwagnen). You need to know when the whole orchestra should be playing together, and when to bring in certain sections or combinations of sections. You need to plan for how many players you'll need in each section, and plan for the pieces you'll be playing in future concert seasons in addition to the ones you're currently playing. You need to understand your resources—do you need a percussionist who can play everything from tympani to vibraslap, or can you afford to have one person whose entire job it is to hit the triangle once per performance? And you should be aware of your own strengths and weaknesses, so that you can have musicians who complement them. You are the CEO of your orchestra.

Pick whatever team-building metaphor seems best tailored to your tastes. But to build an effective team, you need to look at not just the individuals you hire, but at the broader picture of what you need the whole organization to accomplish. For example, we all want creative heavy hitters on our team. But ask yourself whether that rockstar will complement the team's capabilities, create redundancy, or even create resentment. They may be great, but are they great for you? Don't just think about what you need now, determine where you want to lead the team. Consider how many more hires you are going to get to make in the coming year and how to optimize each hire you make. And think about where the team is headed, and the overall skills you'll need the team to have to get there. What kind of creative will you want to do? What new media might you expand into? What new clients might you pitch? Play the long game. That is not a sports metaphor.

Build A Portfolio Of Talent

The second most important thing I can tell you about building a team is to always have people lined up who you want to hire. Once you've built your system, you need the right people to fill those roles. And you know just how fickle the creative industry is. You may go months without having the opportunity to hire anyone, and then suddenly you win a big assignment and need to hire several people all at the same time. Or you may have an open position that doesn't stay open for long, because someone in finance will start asking questions once the role has been around for longer than 90 days. It's always in your best interest to hire people fast. And the best way to do that is to already have people lined up that you want to hire. A strong

CHAPTER 6 CREATE OPPORTUNITY: HOW TO BUILD YOUR TEAM

pipeline gives you the ability to jump on every creative opportunity, and that sets your team up to be successful.

One of the first, and best, pieces of advice I got when I was a junior writer was to never stop working on my portfolio. I imagine you've heard something similar along the way. As a creative leader, you don't create the work anymore. But you do create the team that will make the work. So now, instead of a building a portfolio of your ads, you are building a portfolio of portfolios. You are building a portfolio of people. And you should never stop working on it.

When you created your first portfolio, the guidance you got probably went something like this: First, you need to make some work. Find the insight that will resonate with your audience. Dig around to find those killer ideas, and kill your darlings. Craft the work to within an inch of its life. Make the copy, the design, and the art direction sing. Sweat the details. Find even better ideas than your last ones. Never stop working on your portfolio.

Include 5–7 campaigns, with 3–5 executions per idea. Cover a variety of products including but not limited to packaged goods, tech, soda, finance, videogames, and retail. Put your best campaigns first, and bury your less favorite ones in the middle. Pick hard or boring products, because anyone can do a great Nike or Apple ad (author's note: not everyone can do a great Nike or Apple ad). Show how your ideas work across media, including film, outdoor, print, social, and nontraditional. Put some radio ideas in there, even though no one will ever listen to them (author's note: I always listen to radio). As you gain experience in the industry and create better and better work, replace the weakest campaigns with stronger ones. Never stop working on your portfolio.

I apply the same logic to building a talent pipeline. Take all of that passion and energy that you poured into your own portfolio, and redirect it toward finding the absolute best talent out there. Instead of poring over award show books for ideas to steal (er, be inspired by), look at who did the work you admire most and see if you love the rest of their portfolios as much as that one killer campaign. Add them to your portfolio of people. When you see a featured campaign in *AdWeek, AdAge, Creativity*, or *Campaign*, find out who wrote, art directed, creative directed, designed, produced, or shot the work. Add them to your portfolio of people. Spend time poking around on talent sites and see whose work speaks to you. Follow industry newsletters, blogs, and podcasts, and gleefully plunder the featured creatives. Find out who did that ad you saw in the subway. Reach out to the heads of placement at ad schools and ask them to send you links to their graduating classes' portfolios—they'll be more than happy to, because they want to see their people get jobs. Reach out to your friends and colleagues in the industry and ask them for recommendations. Go on LinkedIn and plug in senior art director, ACD copywriter, executive producer, media strategist, or any other title you're looking to hire for. Heck, plug those same titles into Google—you know whoever pops up will at least be good at SEO. Keep building that list. Never stop working on your portfolio.

Invest time getting to know the portfolios you've collected. Refine your talent pipeline the way you would your own portfolio. Look for the quality of their ideas, and pay attention to the details of the executions and their craft. Watch their TikToks with the same discerning eye as their TV spots. Read their post copy. Listen to their radio.

I also look to see how people approach the construction of their websites as a proof point for how they approach their work. Did the copywriter write about their ideas with clarity, wit, and emotion? Is the art director's site as beautiful as the work on the site? Is the UX designer's site intuitive and easy to navigate? Does the creative director's site explain how they led their team to make the work? Is their passion for how they present their work as clear as their passion for the work itself? Do they walk the talk?

When I was looking for the first head of production for my team at LinkedIn, I started asking around. There was one person whose name came up more than once—already a good sign. When I reached out to this

CHAPTER 6   CREATE OPPORTUNITY: HOW TO BUILD YOUR TEAM

person to see if she wanted to learn more about the role and my team, she started by telling me all about what she had already heard about the team I was building. Then she started sharing ideas about how she would help me approach building it. *Then* she told me about my team's projects that she had seen her buddies at a local editing house working on, and offered up suggestions for how to improve the process. She already knew what was going on with my team because she was so connected. And that's one of the things that makes a great producer great—the relationships they've built in the production world, and the depth and breadth of those connections. That's how they get the absolutely most bang out of every single production dollar. And that's what I knew I needed in a head of production. Before I ever saw a single spot she had produced, before we ever met in person, I put her up front in my talent portfolio because she walked the talk.

In the same way that you showcased different ideas for different clients in different media in your own portfolio, you'll want to have people with a variety of different strengths, backgrounds, and levels in your talent portfolio. Just like you'd have a TV campaign, a social campaign, an outdoor campaign, and an integrated campaign, you'll want people who are great at TV, social, outdoor, and integrated campaigns. You'll want writers and art directors and designers of all levels. And if you oversee people besides creatives, you'll want producers, traffic people, strategists, media people, and all of the subdisciplines that go with them. Make sure you have a diverse talent pool (more on diversity in a bit). Like the killer campaigns in your creative portfolio lead to better assignments or new jobs, the killer people in your talent portfolio lead to better work and attract more great people. As you find better and better people, move them to the top of your list. Remove the people whose work doesn't inspire you anymore. Make your talent portfolio sing like your own portfolio. Make a talent portfolio that your coworkers and colleagues would be jealous of. Make a talent portfolio that would win an award if there was an award for

CHAPTER 6   CREATE OPPORTUNITY: HOW TO BUILD YOUR TEAM

talent portfolios (The Jobbies? The Hirees? The Bookies?). Repeat and refine the process. Never stop working on your portfolio.

Like your creative portfolio, your people portfolio isn't tied to any particular agency. You take it from job to job, and as you become more experienced your work gains depth and breadth. As you advance in your creative leadership roles, your responsibilities will grow. You may only have the opportunity to hire one person at first, but you'll need to hire more and more as you get more senior and oversee more teams. Just like you grew your portfolio of creative work, keep growing your portfolio of creative people. Have a full pipeline. And say it with me now:

Never stop working on your portfolio of people.

One important advantage that people have over work in a portfolio is that you can talk to people. You can build relationships with them. As tidy as the analogy of a portfolio of work and a portfolio of people is, I've got another one for how to build and maintain those relationships:

Look for a potential employee like you are looking for a potential employer.

In the same way you'd reach out to an agency recruiter or CCO, reach out to the people on your list of talent. Introduce yourself. Send them a simple, complimentary note saying not just that you think their work is exciting, but also what you found to be so specifically exciting about it. Because who doesn't like hearing that you thought their work was cool? Nobody, that's who. Acknowledge that they might not be looking for a new job right now, but ask for an informational interview. Spend a few minutes saying hi, learning about the projects they've worked on, what they're passionate about, and what they might like to do next. Share what you and your team have been up to. Ask them what success looks like for them. Ask their permission to stay in touch if something opens up down the road, and ask their permission to follow up every few months to see if there are any new developments. Follow up with them every few months

CHAPTER 6 CREATE OPPORTUNITY: HOW TO BUILD YOUR TEAM

as promised to build the relationship. Thank them for their time. In other words, do exactly what you'd do when you're looking for a new job.

When you're a creative leader, you've got to get good at playing the long game. I once stumbled across a portfolio site of a mid-level art director whose work I thought was both beautiful and insightful. I reached out to him, and thanks to the miracle of modern technology I have the actual conversation archived.

> May 31, 6:37 pm
> Hey (art director's name withheld to protect the innocent), I think your work is really solid. What're you up to these days? Kevin
>
> June 1, 2:42 pm
> Hey Kevin, I'm currently about to travel for production for the next month or so, but I'm not actively looking to leave (agency name withheld to protect the innocent) as of yet. But I'd love to grab coffee sometime when I'm back.
>
> June 1, 5:01 pm
> Awesome, have a great shoot. give me a shout when you're back. Kevin
>
> FOUR AND A HALF MONTHS LATER
>
> October 19, 8:25 am
> Hey, want to get that coffee sometime soon? Kevin
>
> October 19, 9:45 am
> Hi Kevin! Sure, let's grab a coffee sometime soon. Are you free next week?
>
> October 19, 4:42 pm
> How about Monday at 10?
>
> FIVE MONTHS LATER
>
> March 12, 11:44 am
> Hey Kevin, we never got to have that coffee, shall we try again sometime soon?

CHAPTER 6   CREATE OPPORTUNITY: HOW TO BUILD YOUR TEAM

March 12, 8:50 pm

Hey, been meaning to reach out to you. I'm traveling for work this week, what's next week/week after look like for you?

SIX WEEKS LATER

April 25

Hey Kevin! I'm checked in and in the lobby.

During that first meeting, I asked him lots of questions. More than just what he was working on, but what he was passionate about. Where he wanted to take his career next, and what skills he hoped to learn. I asked him what he thought he needed to be successful. And I told him about where our team was in its development and growth. I let him know about the exciting things that we had going on, and was transparent about the challenges we were facing and where we needed his help. And I gave him lots of time to ask questions, which he had a lot of and which I answered as honestly as I could.

A position had also opened up during the months between when I first reached out and our initial meeting. He came in to officially interview with the rest of my team the next week, but my mind was already made up. And I like to think that his was too. He knew what he was getting into, he knew that I appreciated what he was bringing to the team, and he knew what kind of leadership he could expect from me. He accepted our offer on May 22, nearly one year to the day after I first reached out. The time I had invested keeping him in my pipeline over the past year had paid off. Playing the long game led to a great hire, and he stayed on the team for nearly four years.

As I build my pipeline, I also share it with my counterparts at other agencies when they call looking for new talent. This might seem counterintuitive in a business that holds its ideas so close to its chest. You've invested so much time in building your portfolio of people, unearthing great work, and meeting the people who dreamed it up. What if they go work for someone else?

Well, what if they do?

CHAPTER 6   CREATE OPPORTUNITY: HOW TO BUILD YOUR TEAM

There are so many reasons to share your pipeline. The more good people who get jobs, the better the work in the industry will become overall, which leads to more growth in the industry, which leads to more jobs (another virtuous cycle!). When you share your pipeline with your colleagues, they're more likely to return the favor down the road—you might not need a mid-level writer right now, but you may find yourself suddenly in need of an account supervisor in six months. The people in your pipeline you make those referrals for won't forget the favor, either. Talented people have talented friends they can add to your pipeline. But more than that, remember, you're playing the long game. In a couple of years, there may be other opportunities for them to join your team. And if they do, they'll be even more motivated to work for you, because they know you've got their best interests at heart. And even if they never end up working for you, maybe they'll recommend somebody who will. In every case, when you share your pipeline you help the people in it to be more successful.

Which, as you know, is your job as a creative leader.

The Interview: Your Very First One-To-One

You've won that new business pitch, or gotten a juicy new assignment, or someone on your team quit, or the headcount gods have otherwise blessed you with the opportunity to hire. Now you're ready to bring in candidates for an official interview. Congratulations! You'll have 30 to 60 minutes to make a decision that will affect your team for years to come. Here's how to make the most of that very limited window.

First, since you've built your talent pipeline so methodically (and I know you have *totally* done that), you'll be much better prepared for an interview. And now that you know the specific role you're hiring for, you can be more specific about how the opportunity matches up with your candidate's career goals. Are there opportunities for them to work on new

CHAPTER 6 CREATE OPPORTUNITY: HOW TO BUILD YOUR TEAM

kinds of clients and projects? Will they be able to extend their skills into new media? Will they be able to get more face time presenting to senior leadership? Will there be opportunities to manage people? See if there's still a good match between the skills the candidate is looking to gain from their next job, and the skills they already have that you need on your team.

It is, as you might have noticed, a whole lot like a one-to-one.

If you can set a person up for growth and success *before* they join your team, they're more likely to feel fulfilled when they actually join your team. They'll be more productive. They'll work harder. They'll be happier. They'll know what to expect from you as a leader.

Treating an interview like a one-to-one will give you a sense of what kind of employee a candidate will be beyond the brilliant campaigns you see in their portfolio. Are they open to new ideas? Are they open to your management style? Do they seem coachable? Are they curious about the work that's happening on your team? Do they want to learn and grow?

Here's my favorite question to ask in an interview, pretty much verbatim:

"Let's say it's four years from now. You pull me aside, and say 'Kevin, we need to talk. It's been a great four years, and I've learned so much. But I just got a call from (insert current hot agency name) and they want me to be their Global CCO.' What do you want to have learned in your time here that will get you to that next level?" I'm walking the talk by showing that their career development is my number one priority—even more than their creativity. I'm also being honest by dispelling any unrealistic expectations that they'd work for me forever. It also gives them the chance to show me that they're thinking about their career, what their priorities are, and how they align with what I'm looking for on my team.

I even share with the candidate how I'm treating the interview as our first one-to-one. I explain what one-to-ones are, my expectations on how we'll approach them, and how my job as a creative leader is to help my team members be more successful—I basically do everything I described in the one-to-one chapter as part of the interview.

In addition to sharing the opportunities on the team, I'm also transparent about the challenges we're facing, and why I need that person's help solving them. I tell them about all of the Giant Hairy Spiders in the team's bathroom. If I've got a particularly tough client that I need help managing, I ask the candidate for ideas on how they'd help managing them. If I need to grow my production budgets, I ask for suggestions on that. If I need to push for bigger, bolder creative ideas for a conservative line of business, I ask how the candidate feels about taking clients out of their comfort zones. I ask the candidate whether they're scared or excited by these challenges (they should be a bit of each). Showing a candidate how they can help makes them feel valued. But more than that, when I'm honest about the hard parts of the job it conveys to a candidate that I'll be on the level with them if they come work on my team. I do my best to walk the talk. And just like in a one-to-one, sharing the ugly underbelly of the job along with the shiny bits helps establish that there will be no surprises along the way. It sets the foundation for your relationship with your employee before they ever start working for you.

How To Create A Successful Team Of Interviewers

Chances are you won't be the only person to interview a candidate. And if you are, you shouldn't be. As a creative leader (and CEO of your team), it's important to consider the input of your colleagues and team members to make informed decisions. This is where having multiple people interviewing a candidate comes in handy.

One quick clarification: when I say have multiple people interview a candidate, I mean have them interview the candidate individually. I never have them interview a candidate at the same time—otherwise known as a panel interview. Even if the members of a panel interview have perfectly choreographed their questions (which they haven't), a panel is disorienting for a candidate. Questions come from all angles. It's more challenging to build rapport with multiple people simultaneously, and there's less opportunity to build a personal connection with the interviewer. There's also more physical space between interviewer and interviewee, which makes the whole experience colder. Somebody inevitably comes late and you have to waste time catching them up. One could argue that the ability to address a group is a skill that you're testing for in a panel, but if you really want to test for that then make a formal presentation part of the process. Let the interview be one-to-one time. It's already nerve-wracking to participate in a process as artificial as an interview, there's no need to make it more stressful. Remember, your job is to help the candidate be more successful, even before their first day on the job.

Now that you've wisely decided on individual interviews over a panel, assign the interviewers on your team clear areas to cover. You can have one person assess conceptual and technical skills. Have someone else explore whether the person is a cultural fit. You can have your team ask about client skills, management skills, or anything else that you're looking for in that role and at that level. Be thoughtful about whom you assign to each role, matching your interviewers to their areas of expertise. Just as the people on your team have different functional areas of expertise in their jobs, they can have different functions in an interview. The reason you want to give everyone a specific area is to make sure you cover everything—if you don't assign your interviewers specific areas, they may all ask about the same thing (or worse, they may ask about nothing). Then when you get feedback from them on different candidates, you'll have a more informed comparison. It's still not an exact science, but at least it's more apples to apples than, say, apples to pandas.

After the interviews are over, ask your interviewing team for a recommendation, and look for consensus. Ask them for objective, observable feedback on a candidate in the areas you've assigned—"I just have a good feeling about this person" shouldn't necessarily be discounted

CHAPTER 6   CREATE OPPORTUNITY: HOW TO BUILD YOUR TEAM

as a reason to hire someone, but it probably shouldn't be the main reason. Ask your team not to talk to each other about their opinions, because that can influence their recommendation (they will likely do this anyway, but it doesn't hurt to ask). See how their input aligns with your own opinions. Who you hire is ultimately your decision, but make it as informed a decision as you can. Just like when you're evaluating work, you always have permission to trust your gut. But it's got to be grounded in the brief.

A couple other nuts-and-bolts interviewing practices: I try to limit my interview team to a maximum of 3 or 4 people. You are setting candidates up for success, and no one is going to have a successful conversation after four and a half hours when they're on the ninth of 12 interviews. Having fewer interviewers also means it's more likely that the candidate will only have to come in once. People are busy, and it takes a lot of juggling to make time to come in and talk to your team. Occasionally you may have to bring a candidate back in to meet bigger cheeses than you, but showing a potential employee that you are respectful of their time is another way to demonstrate that their success is your priority. And speaking of cheese, if you're going to schedule an interview over lunchtime, buy your candidate lunch. Nobody is at their best when they're hungry.

Hire A Diverse Team

I am not a DEI expert. And chances are, neither are you (DEI stands for Diversity, Equity, and Inclusion—even if you're not an expert, you need to know that). And if you do happen to be a diversity expert, I apologize in advance for getting any of this wrong. Anyway, you don't have to be a diversity expert to hire a diverse team.

Diversity is good for its own sake. Helping people from historically underrepresented or outright excluded groups get jobs is good for society. But diversity is also good for creativity. If you only hire one kind of person (say, just hypothetically, straight white males in their late 20's to mid

30's) you're going to get a very limited scope of creative ideas (say, just hypothetically, 30-second TV spots featuring a series of slapsticky, ironic, or otherwise comedic vignettes that are neatly tied up at the end with a title card explaining what you just saw). When you hire people from a variety of backgrounds, you're going to get a wider and richer variety of creative ideas. And your clients have diverse customer bases, so a diverse team will be able to help better connect to those audiences.

Hiring a diverse team is not just good for you, it's good for the entire industry. When people see other people like themselves represented in the jobs they want, particularly at the leadership level, they know that opportunities exist for them to succeed. Which means a more diverse group of people will apply for creative positions, and will get jobs as more creative leaders like you hire them. Which means more diversity in the business. Which means better ideas. Which means growth in the industry. Which means more jobs, and more opportunities to make the industry more diverse. Hey, it's another virtuous cycle!

As you build your team, be mindful of gender, race, age, sexual orientation, and all of the other groups we think of as "traditionally" diverse. But there are other kinds of diversity. Socioeconomic, disability, and neurodiversity, to name a few. There's also diversity in the kinds of roles you're hiring for. The most common example of this in advertising is art directors and writers—we pair them up to get a richer perspective. But a person with a social background is going to solve a problem differently from one with an experiential background. Someone who's experienced the constraints of a small agency will bring a different perspective from a big agency person. A designer will solve a problem differently from a TikTokker. And a junior person may bring a fresher take while a senior person may bring a more informed one.

One other note on diversity: I've often heard the term "diverse person" used as a substitute for a BIPOC individual (BIPOC stands for Black, Indigenous, and People Of Color, and you need to know that too). But individuals are not diverse, groups are. You don't just get to hire a BIPOC individual and consider the problem solved. Look at the overall makeup of your team, and hire a group that is representational of people from different backgrounds.

As a creative leader, one measure of your success is the quality of your creative output. And the best creative comes from a diversity of creative ideas. Which comes from a diverse team.

Bias Is The Enemy Of Diversity

In addition to not being a DEI expert, I am also not an expert on bias. But again, neither you nor I need to be an expert in the subject to be aware of unconscious biases and how they can affect hiring decisions.

Everyone has biases. There are the ones you know about, and the ones you don't. The biases you're not aware of are called, appropriately, unconscious biases.[1] And like I said, you have them. I have them. Everyone does. They can affect your hiring decisions (and lots of other creative decisions) in sneaky and unpleasant ways. It's not hard to draw a straight line between these biases and how they get in the way of hiring a diverse team, which gets in the way of diverse creative ideas.

There's confirmation bias, which is the tendency for people to pay attention to or otherwise favor information that supports the things they already believe. So in the case of hiring a creative person, you might be more likely to like them if you like their work. You can see how this can be dangerous, as there are award-winning campaigns out there made by not-so-award-winning people. There's affinity bias, which means people tend to be drawn to people like themselves. This is how an industry that has historically been white and male stays white and male, and how you get so many of those slapsticky 30-second spots. There's gender bias, in

---

[1] Oberai, Himani, and Ila Mehrotra Anand. "Unconscious Bias: Thinking without Thinking." *Human Resource Management International Digest*, vol. 26, no. 6, 2018, pp. 14–17.

which a person assigns certain attributes to certain genders. Action bias is the tendency for action over inaction, and it can get in the way of diversity when you're under pressure to hire fast (or trying to problem solve when a person just wants to vent). Conformity bias is when people tend to go along with the opinions of others in a group, which is another reason to stay the heck away from panel interviews.

These are just some of the unconscious biases. But the catch-22 with all of them is that since they're unconscious, you don't know about them. And how can you possibly address a thing that you don't know about? All you can really do is be aware that they exist, and accept that you have biases even if you don't think you do. When you make hiring decisions, ask yourself if those decisions could be a result of an unconscious bias. This takes practice and commitment. And if you've got good DEI or recruiting departments, lean on them for guidance. They're your friends and they know more about this stuff than either of us.

A Note On Thank You Notes

As you might have noticed, I place a high a value on saying thank you. And I want people on my team who also understand the value of saying thank you. So I always check whether a person sends me a thank you note after an interview.

A thank you note doesn't have to come in the form of flowers or candy or on personalized stationery. It can be an email that says some version of "Hey Kevin, thanks so much for your time. I'm super psyched to work for you." Though for a creative job, a creative thank you helps make the case. And I end every interview by sharing my email address with a candidate, and by inviting them to email me with any other questions they have. In addition to demonstrating that I'm a supportive leader, it gets around recruiters or coordinators who might not be at liberty to share your contact info. It's a foolproof way to make sure someone knows exactly where to send that thank you note.

CHAPTER 6   CREATE OPPORTUNITY: HOW TO BUILD YOUR TEAM

Do This After You Make An Offer

Congratulations! You've decided on the perfect candidate and offered them a job. At this point, most agencies just sit back and wait for a reply. That's because the creative market is always competitive, and some agencies have a higher opinion of themselves than they should. Don't be that agency.

Instead, send the candidate a separate note saying how excited you are at the prospect of them joining your team. Tell them you know this is a big decision, and you'll be available to answer any questions so they can make the right decision. Remember, you're letting them know what to expect from you as a leader before their first day on the job. You spent all that time deciding they were the right person. You want them to work for you.

If they accept your offer, send them another note telling them how excited you are. Yes, another one. Everyone wants to hear their future boss say how thrilled they are that they'll be part of the team. And if they don't accept your offer, send them a note. Yes, another one. Thank them for their time. Tell them how grateful you are to have had the opportunity meet them. Invite them to keep in touch. Keep them in your portfolio of people, because you never know, they still might want to work for you someday.

Or you might want to work for them.

Firing People Sucks

Hopefully, you're building your team with an eye to the future. You're bringing on people who have skills that are transferrable across a variety of situations. But the needs of your company and your clients are constantly evolving, and if you don't have the right people in place when change happens it leaves you with an unenviable choice. You have to decide

CHAPTER 6   CREATE OPPORTUNITY: HOW TO BUILD YOUR TEAM

whether you can train the people on your existing team to address the changing demands of the business, or you need to make room to hire others who have the skills you need to get the job done.

I'm going to pause here to ask this question again: Are you *sure* you want to lead a creative team? Because there's no shame in just continuing to be a creative. And firing people is a lot less fun than being a creative.

I'm not talking about firing people for cause. If you've got someone on your team who is throwing chairs in client meetings, or doing lines off the conference room table, or making sexually suggestive remarks about a co-worker, or otherwise acting in a manner that's inappropriate or illegal, show them the door. I mean letting perfectly capable and nice people go because they just aren't the right fit for what you need to be a successful leader. Your business has evolved, but they haven't.

Some companies let you make a clean break with an employee. If you have that option, I highly recommend you take it. It's not fun, but at least it's quick. Other companies, particularly if you work brand-side, may require you to "manage out" an employee. For a process that has a lot of cringeworthy euphemisms (we're letting you go, we're ending our relationship, we're downsizing, we're reorganizing, it's not you it's us), this is one of the cringeworthiest. Managing out is an approach where you gather feedback that demonstrates an employee is not succeeding in their role, and set tough new goals based on that feedback. It may seem more humane on the surface, but it's a long, drawn-out process with a foregone conclusion. If you do have to manage someone out, chances are you work at a place that has clear guidelines and HR will have a heavy hand in the whole thing. Follow their lead.

In either case, be as compassionate as you can. Be honest with your employee about where your team is headed, and why you have to let them go. Answer their questions as honestly as you can. Give them space to get as emotional as they want. They are going to be frustrated. They are going to be confused. They are going to be angry. They may want to yell at you.

CHAPTER 6   CREATE OPPORTUNITY: HOW TO BUILD YOUR TEAM

Let them. If you've been let go yourself (and chances are you have, given the business we work in), tell them you know how they feel. Offer them as much severance as you can. Offer to make introductions to your friends and colleagues in the industry who can help them out. Thank them. Mean it.

Even in an unpleasant situation, your job as a creative leader is still to help people be more successful. So you can gently suggest that in this case, maybe success is leaving a job that's not the right fit anymore. They'd probably be happier, and more successful working somewhere else. And while it's a hard thing to say, at least it's the truth.

Firing people sucks. If you hire people who can flex and grow with your team, you'll have to do it less. But you'll still have to do it eventually. And hopefully you'll be able to build a more successful team as a result of those hard decisions.

I Am All Up In My Hiring Process' Business

Just in case it's not obvious, I have been very hands-on with building my teams. I'll have more to say in the next chapter on how hands-on you can and should be in another crucial part of your job, but my grubby little fingerprints are all over my hiring process all the time. The ideas you create will only be as good as the people on your team who are creating them. So I spent a lot of my time looking at portfolios and curating my talent pipeline. Even when I had the luxury of a creative manager or recruiter to help source talent, I still paid close attention to portfolio sites, awards shows, trade publications, blogs, colleagues, ad school sites, and all of the other places I might find talented people. I made sure I had a diverse talent pool. I personally obsessed over it in the same way I obsess over every single piece of work in my own portfolio. And I met every single candidate from the biggest wig right down to the greenest, freshest out of ad school, junior-est junior. Me. Myself.

CHAPTER 6   CREATE OPPORTUNITY: HOW TO BUILD YOUR TEAM

"But Kevin," you say, "Where did you find the time to do all of that?"

I made time.

As a creative leader, you don't create the work anymore. You create the team.

Because you are the CEO of your team.

CHAPTER 7

Create Creative: How To Give Feedback And Direction

When you're not having one-to-ones, building culture, looking for future team members, managing stakeholders, saying thank you, or otherwise busy with all of the stuff you might not have realized a creative leader does, it turns out you have to do the part of the job you thought you signed up for: giving creative direction. It also turns out that you may not be very good at it. And that's OK. You probably haven't been taught how to give creative feedback or may not have given creative feedback at all, and it's likely that you haven't been given good direction yourself. Most creative directors tell their teams what to do, without ever telling them why it's important or how they'd like to see the feedback implemented. So you're stuck in a vicious cycle of creative directors who aren't good at giving direction creating more creative directors who also aren't good at it. So, why are people who are so good at being creative so bad at giving creative direction?

Giving creative feedback is scary.

That's because human beings have feelings, and giving feedback runs the risk of hurting them. On top of that, creative people are notorious for our heightened emotions—the same natural passion and empathy that

CHAPTER 7   CREATE CREATIVE: HOW TO GIVE FEEDBACK AND DIRECTION

draws us to the business also makes us especially sensitive to giving and receiving feedback. We've poured our hearts and souls into the work, and it sucks to have to tell the people you care about that their work needs to be changed. So rather than risk hurting a fellow creative, many creative directors (and clients, and colleagues, and everybody else) shy away from giving clear feedback. Or worse, giving any feedback at all.

On the other side of the spectrum, there are creative directors who have no qualms about squishing feelings like bugs under their designer sneakers. Their feedback typically comes in the form of "this is crap," "my dog could do a better ad than this," or (unceremoniously tears the work from the wall and storms out). And even if the CD slips an explanation into the feedback ("my dog could do a better ad than this *because* he understands the insight that people aged 34-52 aren't motivated by weight loss, they want the promise of a healthier lifestyle"), the damage is done. When a creative team feels shamed and demotivated by bad feedback, it shows up in the work.

Without good feedback delivered well, everyone suffers. Your team misses opportunities to grow and learn. A great idea that just needed a push in the right direction to get a thumbs up from the client dies because the CD is afraid to give it that push. A mediocre idea that should have been killed slips through and gets produced, setting off a vicious cycle of the client wanting more ideas equally as mediocre, the agency forced to choose making those mediocre ideas over losing the client, and the client eventually leaving anyway for an agency that makes better work. I told you creative people were especially sensitive.

So, how do you give feedback to people who take feedback so personally? Approach your creative reviews the way you approach your one-to-ones. Show that you care as much about the work as you do about the people doing the work.

Set the work up for success.

CHAPTER 7   CREATE CREATIVE: HOW TO GIVE FEEDBACK AND DIRECTION

Before You Give A Lick Of Feedback Part 1: Give Direction

You may recall that your whole job as a creative leader is to help your people be more successful. You established it in your very first one-to-ones with each of your team members. And as a result, you built the foundations for healthy relationships. You created a safe space to share positive and negative feedback about their professional development. By approaching the creative process in a similar way, you're making a safe space to share feedback about the development of the work.

Just like in your first one-to-one, you need to be clear about your role and your expectations up front. Start with the same powerful phrase: I am here to make the work more successful. Then you need to set goals. And that means giving direction in the briefing, before the team puts pen to paper. A kickoff meeting isn't just for the strategist to strategize and the account people to account—it's for the creative director to give direction. That means you need to be proactive. Give yourself plenty of time before the briefing to think about the assignment. Then show up with three or four areas for the creatives to explore. And just like a one-to-one, it's not a one way street. Give your team the opportunity to brainstorm other directions with you, and agree on the ones you want to pursue. Take time to brainstorm new directions with the team that you all agree are worth pursuing. Then, when you get to the first creative review, everyone will be on the same page. It's the first step of a successful process.

On the other hand, when you don't give direction up front, it sets up a vicious cycle. We've all been in briefings where the creative team gets the assignment, and then is sent off to crank up the idea machine without a word from the creative director. Fast forward to the first creative review. The team is excited to share what they've been working so hard on, nervous because they're putting a piece of themselves up on the wall, and hoping for praise and approval from the creative director. They start flipping through ideas. After explaining why each is on brief and why they're so excited about them, they exhale, and wait silently. Hopefully, there are ideas that the CD likes. But sometimes, the CD will say this:

"Well, I was thinking something more like…"

In a single stroke, the CD has wasted an entire review cycle and taken the wind out of the team's sails. The team has to start again. And in the next round, the work will suffer because the team is up against a shorter timeline and because they're feeling demotivated. Not to mention that the team feels like they didn't have input into the ideas in the first place.

I know that some leaders explain this approach away by saying it gives the team more creative freedom. But often it's just because the creative director hasn't taken the time to think through the creative direction—it's easier to be reactive in the second review than proactive in the first. It's another version of the infamous "I don't know what I want, but I'll know it when I see it" client comment that drives creatives up the wall. And as a creative leader, it is definitely not your job to drive your people up the wall. Give the team room to play, but give it to them within the boundaries you've agreed to in the kickoff meeting.

When you get to the first creative review, start off conversationally just like in your one-to-ones. Take five minutes to share something that's going on in your personal life, and ask the teams about work-appropriate things you know are going on in theirs. And yes, I know that reviews often start late, and there's never enough time to talk about the work. But investing time in conversation up front is well worth it. Showing interest in your team's personal lives and trusting them with details of yours builds connections. So when you're giving creative feedback a wee bit later, they'll understand it comes from a place of caring.

Then, before anyone presents anything, remind the team that your job is to help the work be more successful (yes, again). And just like in your one-to-ones, establish what success means for the work. The work needs to make the viewer feel something. It needs to make them laugh, cry, cheer, or bring them to their feet with resounding applause. The work needs to be on brand. It needs to be on strategy. It needs to be beautiful. It needs to make the client say yes. Because that's the team's common goal—everyone wants to sell the ideas that they're so passionate about.

That's creating opportunities for the work to be successful.

Before You Give A Lick Of Feedback Part 2: Say Thank You And Empathize

After the team has shared their ideas, thank them for their hard work. But more than that, show that you understand the creative challenges that they faced along the way. Start with a little something like this:

"Thank you for all of your hard work. I know first-hand how challenging it can be when you're (working with a brief that changed for the twentieth time, up against such an insane timeline, dealing with a complicated set of tech specs, dealing with such a crazy creative leader) but you handled it gracefully."

Many creative directors (and account people, and strategists, and clients, and their spouses, and their pets) skip right to the part about all the things they would change, without ever acknowledging the team's efforts. As a creative leader, you have the experience to empathize with the creative process in the same way you empathize with the professional and personal challenges people bring you in your one-to-ones. You're on the team's side. You're one of them. And that helps them to understand that your feedback will be coming from a good place.

Now, you'll notice that I didn't include a healthy heaping of praise as part of that thank you. And that's not because you shouldn't praise your team. It's because too many leaders reflexively say how great they think the work is, even if they don't think it's that great. They're afraid that if they don't, they'll hurt the team's feelings. But false praise is worse than none at all. Your team is looking to you for creative guidance. When you praise everything, they won't learn what you think is good work. It hinders their creative growth. Worse, false praise can undermine the relationship with your team. If you say that you think the work is great, but then you kill it or change it to the point where the original idea is lost, you'll lose your team's trust. We've all heard "I love it, change everything" from clients. The team doesn't ever need to hear it from you. So yes, if you think the work is great, gush away. Otherwise, thank them for the work and acknowledge how much effort they put into it. That's always genuine.

Before You Give A Lick Of Feedback Part 3: Ask Questions

Next, seek to understand as much as you can about why the team made their creative choices. Again, this is the same approach you've used in your one-to-ones. If someone comes to you with a challenge they're facing with their professional development, you're not going to jump straight to the solution. You're going to have a conversation to learn more about the situation. The same thing applies when you're giving creative feedback. Asking questions helps you make better decisions.

Leaders don't need to have all the answers, but they should always have lots of questions.

Before you jump in with what you like, what you'd change, and what you'd kill, learn what went into the work. Start at a high level, and then get granular. Ask why the team took a particular creative approach. Ask how their ideas tie to the strategy and the insight. Ask how the ideas relate to the markets they'll appear in. Ask how the ideas can scale up or down with the budget. Ask how they could work across different media. Ask the team why they chose certain colors, photography styles, or typefaces. Ask about the user experience of a site, and what happens when you click or tap on a button. Ask how they envision producing a spot, what directors they'd use, the pace of the editing, and the style of the music.

Leaders are curious. Asking questions also communicates to your team that you're not just there to pass judgment on the work they've so thoughtfully crafted. You are continuing to empathize with their process. You want to be thoughtful about the feedback you're about to give, and help the work be successful.

OK, *Now* You Can Finally Give Feedback. But...

After you've invested the time to increase your understanding of the work, it's time to give feedback. And, when at last, that time arrives, continue to focus on what will make the work more successful. Not what you like or don't like. Not what you'd hoped to see. Not an idea you came up with that you like better. Not that you wanted it to be red instead of green. When you base your feedback on your own preferences, you're micromanaging. It sets you at odds with your team. Your art director chose that particular shade of green because they loved it. Your writer thought that headline was the cleverest combination of words that have ever been arranged into a sentence. The team is not bringing you work they don't like. So if you like red better than green, or prefer a slightly different shade of green, it's your taste against theirs. Don't make feedback about you.

Instead, make your feedback about developing the work. Start with the phrase "I think the work will be more successful if..." Cover the broad strokes first, then focus on the details. Talk to your team about the things that are working, and the things you want them to change to make the work more successful.

And tell them why.

CHAPTER 7   CREATE CREATIVE: HOW TO GIVE FEEDBACK AND DIRECTION

Overcommunicating Why

Expecting your team to make exactly the same choices that you would is not only unrealistic, it's just plain crazy. But expecting your team to understand how you *think* about the work, and why you make choices when you give direction is a sign of strong creative leadership. That's why sharing the reasons behind your feedback in painstaking detail is as important as the feedback itself. When you tell your team the why behind your feedback, it helps them to have a deeper understanding of what's going on in the business. That knowledge will make the current project tighter and more sellable, and will inform the creative decisions the team makes on future projects. It not only helps the work develop, it helps the team develop.

Leaving out the why can also have negative consequences for your team. It's another pointy-toothed creature that might curl its furry little body around their shins, but also might have them for a light appetizer. Remember, in the absence of an explanation, humans are hard-wired to assume that the unknown will hurt them. When you don't explain to your team why you want to change something, the natural assumption that millions of years of evolution have built into their brains is that you hate them, you hate their work, and they will certainly be fired for their incompetence. Explaining the reasons behind your feedback helps calm the panic in their primal limbic cortices. It adds to the creation a safe environment for your team, and that leads to them being more productive and bringing in better ideas.

Why say why? It helps to make the work more successful. And it helps to make your team more successful.

And with that, I give you a little something I call **Kevin's 10 Whys Of Creative Feedback.**

CHAPTER 7   CREATE CREATIVE: HOW TO GIVE FEEDBACK AND DIRECTION

Why #1: It Made You Feel Something

People don't make purchase decisions because companies argue them into submission. It starts with an emotional attachment to the product or the company. People feel before they think. So before you give the team any rational, left brain-based feedback, notice how the work made you feel. Did it make you laugh? Did it surprise you? Did it scare you? Did you get riled up? Did you get choked up? Did it make you see the world in a different way? Great creative makes people feel something.

That's not to say that there shouldn't be rational reasons behind your feedback, and I'm about to unleash a whole Aristotelian barrage of them. Also, how the work makes you feel is different from what you like. There's a time and a place for your subjective feedback, and I'll get into that as well. When you give creative feedback, you want to give smart, detailed, well-reasoned direction. You need to lead with your head.

But first, lead with your heart.

Why #2: The Brand

The greatest brands in the world have a clear vision of what they stand for. They make more than products, they give you reasons to believe in those products. Apple makes iThings, but they stand for innovation and simplicity. Nike makes sneakers, but they stand for the idea that everyone is an athlete. Coke makes fizzy sugar water, but they stand for happiness. Disney made my house overflow with princess crap for a few years, but they stand for magic.

A strong brand is a powerful why you can give your team. In fact, it can be so powerful I'm going to say something that will get me in trouble with my planner friends:

If you have a great brand, you don't need a great brief.

CHAPTER 7   CREATE CREATIVE: HOW TO GIVE FEEDBACK AND DIRECTION

Now, I'm not saying that I don't value a brief (and hopefully that will win back one or two of those planners). But there's a reason people say that anyone can write a great Nike spot. It's because Nike's brand values are so consistently expressed and so deeply ingrained in popular culture that we all know what to expect from the company. And it doesn't matter if they're talking about running sneakers, soccer cleats, tennis skirts, swim suits, yoga pants, or t-shirts. They start with the belief everyone is an athlete, from the person who's taking their first steps toward getting in shape to the GOATs of their respective sports.

In nearly eight years at Apple, I saw a whole lot fewer creative briefs than one would expect. Now, to be fair, I saw a lot of product marketing briefs. But they were dense documents mostly filled with tech specs, features, and occasionally specific ways the product marketing team wanted those features demonstrated. There were no consumer insights, no target audiences, or any of the other information that would make them recognizable as creative briefs to the average agency person. But there didn't need to be. What it meant to be Apple—what the company looked like, what it felt like, how it acted—was part of the culture. You breathed it in the air. There were no written brand guidelines. The brand existed purely in the minds and hearts of the people who worked on it. It took months, and sometimes years to fully internalize what the company was all about. But when you got it, you lived it. Would the work have been even stronger with traditional creative briefs? Maybe. But because the brand is so strong, everyone knows an Apple ad when they see one. Even if not everyone could write one.

My first encounter with a strong brand came way before Apple. At one of my first agency jobs, I worked on SC Johnson. They were a very different kind of company, but had equally strong conviction in their values. Household cleaning products, bug spray, and plastic wrap were more than packaged goods. They were an education in the power of brand.

CHAPTER 7   CREATE CREATIVE: HOW TO GIVE FEEDBACK AND DIRECTION

SC Johnson is all about family—it's so central to their beliefs that they've got "a family company" locked up with the company name (they've since added "at work for a better world," which I would not have advised had they asked me, but that's a topic for a different book). I once got a brief for Glade PlugIns about how they cover up unpleasant odors. And believe you me, the fart scripts flowed freely (I told you it was one of my first jobs). While those scripts have been mercifully lost to the sands of time, I imagine there was something in there about how Glade covers up even the worst odors that your family can produce (cue grandpa, cue the dog). The work was on brief. It was based in the truth of shared experience. One could even argue that the work was on brand because it was about family. But one would not argue that case successfully. When SCJ says they are a family company, they mean it in the traditional, Rockwellian sense. They are run by a family, they care for each other like family, and they care for their customers like family. So their marketing reflects the brand truth that families love each other unconditionally. They help each other out. And they certainly don't shame each other for clearing the room with a noxious rump-monster. When my CD gave me feedback describing why my work wasn't on brand, he was 100% right. He helped me to understand the client's business, make my next round of work stronger, and to be smarter about assignments down the road. Plug it in, plug it in.

Sometimes, a company has such strongly ingrained brand values that they can only express them as a function of the company itself. The kind of feedback you'll hear in this case is that the work isn't Company Namey: it's not Appley, it's not Googly, it's not Starbucksy, it's not Cloroxy, it's not Bristol Myers Squibby enough. Flash back to the same junior-ish job where I was still learning about the value of a strong brand from SCJ. I got a Quaker Oats assignment where they were launching a Breakthrough Innovation In Dry Breakfast Cereal Bags (I know, I know). Anyway, the bag inside the box came with a zip top to keep the cereal fresher longer.

CHAPTER 7   CREATE CREATIVE: HOW TO GIVE FEEDBACK AND DIRECTION

Naturally, I wrote a spot about a guy sitting at a breakfast table, going on and on excitedly about how great it is that his cereal comes in a zipper, and how important zippers are in general. At the end of his rant, he stands up and the big reveal is that his fly is unzipped. I told you I was still learning.

There are a lot of reasons we should not have presented this idea to the client. But it slipped through, and their reaction (after a long and awkward silence) to what I was sure was the funniest spot ever written was this:

"It's not really Quakery enough."

Now, they weren't wrong. But it also wasn't feedback that I could act on. If I had been the client (or the CD), my feedback would have gone more like this: Quaker is a company that stands for wholesomeness. We don't just make oatmeal and granola bars, we give people the opportunity to lead a more healthy lifestyle and feel better about themselves. So take your little zipper joke and shove it up your fart-hole.

Sorry, still learning.

Many companies have formalized their brand values into written guidelines. These are a useful resource, because they can help take the guesswork out of Company Namey feedback. A good brand book will provide high-level guidance around the company's beliefs and guiding principles, as well as how those values will show up in the execution of the work.

When we created the brand guidelines at LinkedIn, we were fighting the perception that the company was cold and impersonal. That wasn't any big surprise—many of the people on the platform were a homogeneous group of white collar professionals, and the marketing was a cold sea of blue, white, and black. One of our goals in creating the guidelines was to humanize the brand—to warm it up.

We designed the guidelines with that principle in mind. We outlined a conversational and jargon-free style of copy. We used a palette that leaned into the warmer end of the color spectrum. We created a typeface that used rounded letters. We created our own photo library that used real people

CHAPTER 7   CREATE CREATIVE: HOW TO GIVE FEEDBACK AND DIRECTION

in real business situations, with nary a fake conference room high-five to be found. Having brand guidelines was an objective source of truth. It streamlined the feedback process. It saved time and money, and eased tensions over individual tastes.

The guidelines clearly defined what it meant to be Linked-Inny.

So, while Comic Sans will always be the king of fonts, a proprietary typeface in the brand guidelines is a clear reason why you're giving feedback to change it. And let's go back to that shade of green that your art director just looooved (it was Pantone 2256, in case you were wondering). Well, it's not in the brand book. And neither was the red that you liked, smarty-pants. And while I might like fart jokes, if the brand tone says otherwise then those deadly little stinkers need to be silenced. In every case, there's a clear reason why you're steering the work toward a solution that's more on-brand.

I know as a creative it's easy to demonize brand guidelines as too restrictive. And many brands don't even have guidelines. But none of that matters. You can't fight the brand. As a creative leader, you need to embrace it. Internalize it. That's how to achieve the "true partnership" with clients that we all promise in pitches. The brand is a clear reason why you're giving feedback, and you'll create work that's more successful.

Why #3: Your Agency Has A Brand Too

Your clients hired your agency to help them build their brands. But they also hired you because of your agency's brand. Luckily for you, most agencies have their beliefs painted in foot-high letters in their foyers, animated on their homepages, nailed to their doors, or toothily grinning down from black flags above their headquarters. And hopefully, the whole reason you and your team took jobs at the agency was because their philosophy was aligned to yours. If your agency has positioned itself as a disruptor, the work should be unexpected, mischievous, or shocking.

If your shop is known for humor, some guts better be a-busting. Are you folksy? Data-driven? Ironic? Conservative? Are you a ragtag bunch of scrappy underdogs? Uncompromising perfectionists? Pirates?

You are a steward of your agency's brand every bit as much as you are of your client's brand. Giving feedback that brings the work in line with your agency positioning helps the work, and the whole agency, be more successful.

Why #4: The Brief

Your number one source of objective truth is the brief. And you need a tight brief to make the work great. But you knew that. What you may not have realized is that as a creative leader, your relationship to the brief has evolved.

As a maker, you became skilled at identifying what makes a good brief, and what was going to cause trouble down the road. You raised an eyebrow when the target audience was Everyone. You learned to push back when the answer to "what's the one thing that will resonate" was actually a bunch of things strung together with ands in one long sentence. And you learned that there's nothing brief about a ten page brief. As a maker, you learned that to do great creative, you need consumer insights based in truth, a clear strategy, and deliverables you can execute. And you made some noise about it.

But now, my leaderly friend, you can't just poke holes in the brief. It's on you to make sure it's as tight as a Memphis horn section. And the way to do that is to leverage the relationships you've built. Partner closely with your strategists, your account team, and your media people. Get in good with the data scientists, learn to speak their language, and make sure their numbers support the insight. Embrace spreadsheets. Suggest language you think the creative team will understand when leveraging the bandwidth synergy gets too bleeding edge. Listen to your team's input on what would help them make the work better. And when the client adds another thing to

CHAPTER 7   CREATE CREATIVE: HOW TO GIVE FEEDBACK AND DIRECTION

their One Thing, use your one-to-one time to help them understand how a tighter brief will lead to better work. Problem solve together. You need to craft and sell the brief every bit as much as you craft and sell the work.

Now, let's go back to the part about when you were making stuff for a sec. And let's be honest, even with all that noise you were making about tight strategy, sometimes you came up with an idea that wasn't on brief. And you knew it. But you loved it so much you pushed it forward anyway. Some creatives have even been known to do this with ideas about zippers and cereal. But now that you're a creative leader, you don't have that luxury anymore. You need to do more than keep the work on brief, you need to be ruthless about it.

Luckily, being ruthless shouldn't be as hard as the word might suggest. It's your brief, after all. You helped to guide its creation. You managed your stakeholders and came out the other side with a document you are confident will lead to good work. So if the work isn't on brief, it's your responsibility to call it out. It's your credibility on the line.

When you give feedback, share the thinking that led to the brief, and why the things in it are important. If the team has ideas that can be adapted to the brief, give them feedback about how they can push the work to be more strategically sound. Better yet, give them the opportunity to solve it themselves. But when there's no way to make an idea fit, then you need to kill it.

Yes, even if you love it.

Why #5: The Consumer

Agencies complain that clients want to take away their creative freedom. That they don't understand the value or the power of creativity. That all they care about are CTAs, CPCs, RTBs, and ROIs. Clients complain that agencies are so focused on being creative that they are neglecting their business problems. That they just want to slip a goat into their ad or make

CHAPTER 7   CREATE CREATIVE: HOW TO GIVE FEEDBACK AND DIRECTION

ironic mustache jokes. Having worked both on the agency side and the client side, I can say that both make valid points. But who's right?

Neither. The customer is right. Always.

Every agency creative has the gift of empathy. You rose to leadership because you have an exceptional capacity for it. You know how to make the emotional connections with your customers that make them love your work and buy what you're selling. Channel that empathy when you're giving feedback, and challenge your teams to imagine how a consumer will feel when they experience the work.

The good news is we're all consumers. And we all know what a terrible experience feels like. The site that advertises free delivery on all orders over $100 but prices everything at $99.99. Getting added to email lists even after you deliberately unchecked the 'send me marketing emails' box. Retailers that promise every* item is on sale but that asterisk says *most items not on sale. 1-800-CALL-NOW, that's 1-800-CALL-NOW, that number again is 1-800-CALL-NOW, 1-800-CALL-NOW. Mobius strip phone trees. Websites overrun by pop-up windows. Claims that run the gamut from white lies to career politician: The product will keep you dry and odor-free for 96 hours. You'll get a thousand qualified leads with the touch of a button. The sneaker makes you run faster. The airline cares about your travel experience. Anything involving crypto.

Even worse is when the consumer is already engaged, and a company still insists on talking instead of listening:

BLUE BUTTON: Click here to buy

CONSUMER: Awesome! I have done a lot of research and am feeling confident and happy about my decision!

The consumer clicks the blue button

BLUE BUTTON: Do you want to learn more about the product?

CONSUMER: No thanks. I just want to buy it please.

BLUE BUTTON: Do you want to look at items that other consumers bought with this product?

CONSUMER: I'm good.

BLUE BUTTON: How about the terms and conditions?

CONSUMER: Looks super fun, but I'm going to check out your competitors now.

POP-UP WINDOW: Here are some other products we make that you should buy!

When the experience is designed for the seller and not the customer, everybody loses.

Luckily, we all know what a great customer experience feels like too. And I'm going to give a shout out to my UX peeps here. For those of you who haven't worked as interactive creatives, there is an entire discipline called user experience, and they fight for the forces of good on the web. Their whole job is to imagine things from the consumer's point of view. When I was leading an interactive team for the first time, I had to learn a whole lot about UX. The value of designing wireframes and building prototypes. How to map out a user flow. The importance of a table read of the entire site. What the heck an AB test was. But most of all, I learned this:

User Experience isn't just for the web.

As a creative leader, approach every assignment—not just web assignments—with the customer's experience at the center. Make prototypes for every project. Mock up a walkthrough of an event. Shoot a rough spot on your phone. Test your insights in focus groups. Put yourself in your customer's shoes every way you can. Ask yourself, and your teams, if the work solves the consumer's problem. If it respects their intelligence. If your message will be welcome or intrusive. If it's useful. If it's helpful. If it's delightful. If that goat is in there because you think goats are funny, or because your client runs a goat farm. When you give feedback from

CHAPTER 7   CREATE CREATIVE: HOW TO GIVE FEEDBACK AND DIRECTION

the point of view of what's best for the customer, it's really what's best for everyone.

Your empathy is your most important prototype.

Why #6: Context

We've all gotten lost in our sketchpads in the heat of creation. But creatives also need to remember that their carefully crafted comps need to live in the real world. So as a creative leader, you need to be mindful of the bigger picture. Give feedback not only on the creative, but how it shows up in different contexts.

If a radio script has 250 words, chances are it's not going to fit in a 60-second spot unless the announcer reads the whole thing at a legal pace. Or a TV script that has 31 "cut to's" in 30 seconds. Or a 20-word billboard headline. Or a website that's designed for a big, beautiful desktop when most users are going to visit it on a cramped mobile screen. If you're going to put your outdoor on top of a taxi, it's going to be speeding by your readers. If it's on a wall downtown, it's probably going to get tagged. If it's on the Nasdaq building in Times Square it's going to have windows poking little black rectangles in it.

As you might expect, Apple was obsessive about context. They wanted to make sure that the experience of buying a product was as considered as the product itself. Back when people lined up around the corner at Apple Stores to get their new phones, we launched a service that let you buy the phone online, and then pick it up on launch day. And those customers were not only guaranteed a new phone, they also got a special line to pick it up. My team's assignment was to create a sign that let those forward-thinking customers know where to line up.

You'd think that'd be an easy one. Slap "If you bought an iPhone online, line up here" on a 36x24 piece of posterboard and move on to the next big marketing challenge. But consider this: If your context happens to be an Apple Store in the UK, then the sign needs to say "If you bought an iPhone online, queue up here." That means another variation, which means more mechanicals and more printing costs and generally more complexity. Also, if you need to translate it to German, which you will, then that headline will get very long, which means you're going to have to come up with a shorter version that fits on the sign. And don't even get me started on Dutch. Fun fact: Muvaffakiyetsizleştiricileştiriveremeyebileceklerimizdenmişsinizcesine is an actual Turkish word. Did I mention you need a simplified Chinese version too? That will only be a couple of characters, so you'll need to look at designs where the type doesn't feel like it's swimming in white space. Oh, and in China you also need to do a different version of the sign for every SKU of the product. So, either you'll need to make a sign for every size, capacity, and color, or create a new sign that can hold all of that information and also be modular to reflect what's in stock on any given day. Got all that? Great, because now you need to run it by legal.

If that makes your head spin, don't worry. That's the process of learning to think about the creative from more than just a creative perspective. But it's well worth the momentary disorientation. Adding the why of context to your feedback helps the team think bigger picture, and that will make everyone more successful.

Why #7: Scale

Sometimes, you'll be in a creative review and the team comes in with an idea that blows you away. It's emotional. It's original. It's dead on strategy. And it costs ten million dollars to produce. Or maybe there's a single small execution in a campaign that you recognize has the potential to be a much bigger idea. When an idea can hold up across different sizes, budgets, media, and markets it's called scalability. This is a powerful selling point. A scalable idea means that a client can test a small version of the idea if they're risk averse, or go all-in with a big budget and not have to worry about spending resources on new ideas for years to come. Scalability solves problems.

I'll use another Apple example to show how scalability works. The Shot on iPhone campaign from TBWA\Media Arts Lab started as an outdoor series. The idea was that the camera was so good that regular people could take great photos on iPhone, and the work would showcase those photos. Since there are a whole lot of regular people in the world, the campaign had a nearly unlimited source of photos to draw from. In addition to those casual photographers, there were professional photographers who wanted to join in the fun. And the kinds of photos that all of those people took on iPhone was another way to scale—stunning landscapes, portraits of friends and family, action shots, food shots, abstracts, the list goes on. Also, everyone in the world speaks photography. So while individual executions needed to be culturally relevant, the idea scaled globally. And by the way, you might have heard about one or two social platforms that people like to post photos on, so the idea leapt off of billboards and into the digital world. But wait, the iPhone also shoots video! Now the campaign could be in even more places, including on good old fashioned television. And after showing all of the beautiful photos and videos you can take on iPhone, we realized that we never actually showed people how to take those beautiful photos and videos. So we created a website that added How to Shoot on iPhone into the Shot on iPhone world.

The idea would have worked as a single billboard. But it didn't have to. When you challenge your team to explore how their ideas can scale, you are literally giving the work the opportunity to grow.

Why #8: The Presentation

Here's another story about Steve that may or may not have actually happened. Once upon a time at the turn of the millennium, Apple was getting ready to launch a product that would change the way the world

CHAPTER 7   CREATE CREATIVE: HOW TO GIVE FEEDBACK AND DIRECTION

listened to music: the iPod. The team had closed in on what they believed would be the final product. So the lead engineer brought it to Steve.

"Eureka!" the engineer cried excitedly, brandishing the rectangle of the purest white. "It's beautiful. It's intuitive. And it can hold 986 songs!" He awaited Steve's approval.

Steve was quiet for a moment, then shook his head solemnly.

"It needs to hold 1,000 songs."

"But…but the technology won't allow 1,000 songs!" stammered the hapless executive.

"It needs to hold 1,000 songs."

"But the silicon RAM ROM megahertz lithium polymer binary technobabble! It's physically impossible!"

"It needs to hold 1,000 songs."

The engineer took a deep breath, and exhaled slowly.

"Why does it need to hold 1,000 songs?"

A hint of a smile kissed the corners of Steve's mouth.

"Because I can't market 986 songs in your pocket."

The moral of the story is that the product and the marketing are more powerful when they're developed at the same time. And the creative is your product.

Think about how you want to sell the creative at the same time as you're developing it. Give feedback with the client presentation in mind, because that's where you're marketing it. Consider how all of the ideas will come together in a cohesive presentation. What's the journey that you want to take your clients on when you share the work? Do you want to start with a positioning line, the research, the insight, or the cultural relevance? Do you want the presentation to suck your clients down the funnel, or float on top with splashy ideas? Maybe you want to bring in a range of emotional work that starts with a belly laugh and ends with open weeping. Or maybe you want to go deep on a particular style, and have the presentation show off your comedic chops from weird as a deodorant campaign to broad as an insurance ad. You may want to have some directions that demonstrate product features and some that lean into product benefits. Or build it like you built your portfolio and put your favorites right up front.

Giving feedback not just on the individual ideas, but also how those ideas come together to shape the presentation lets your team know that you're strategizing around the meeting. You're thinking bigger picture. Your actions teach them about approaching the work from a business standpoint as well as a creative standpoint. It's another way to make the work more successful at the same time as you're helping your team to be more successful.

Why #9: The Execution Needs To Support The Idea

At some point in the feedback process, you're going to have to move from the broad strokes of the idea and dig into the details of the execution. Hopefully, your teams have made choices that are aesthetically pleasing. They're a joy to look at, watch, read, or navigate. But make sure those choices are aligned with the message of the marketing. Let's revisit once again that shade of green that your art director loves. Is it green because it's for a campaign to stop climate change? Does it represent the envy your friends will feel when you cruise by in your shiny new sports car? Are you selling frogs? Or is it green because your art director likes green?

But let's give our art director friend a break for a minute, because we've been picking on her pretty hard. So here's another example. We've all seen the chair that's an aesthetic masterpiece. The one that belongs in a modern art museum more than in your living room. It's made of space-age polymers, or single-origin woods. The lines flow effortlessly, transforming solid material to liquid or making it appearing to float in space. But for all its beauty, there's no way to actually sit in it. And is it even a chair if you can't sit in it? The form of the work needs to follow the function.

Connecting the execution to the idea also allows you to give feedback outside of your area of expertise. I am a copywriter by trade. Which means I am also not an art director, a designer, a coder, an information architect, a producer, or an account person. But I've had to give feedback to team members who are all of those things. So I go back to asking questions about why they made their creative choices, and how those choices support the idea. Even if I don't know the first thing about color theory or grids or diagramming a sentence, I can still give useful feedback to the people who do.

And by the way, when you have to give feedback on things you don't know much about, it gives you the opportunity to learn about them, and show your team that you want to learn about them. Demonstrate that you value their expertise by bringing them into the conversation, instead of making your feedback a one-way street. When you let your team's experience inform your feedback, it's as if the feedback comes from the whole team.

Why #10: Because It's What The Client Would Do

I know the title of this section is going to raise a lot of hackles in the creative community. But consider this:

Clients are going to poke holes in your creative no matter what.

"Go ahead, let them," you might say. "That's their job. I am an awesome creative leader and my job is to blow their minds with my

CHAPTER 7   CREATE CREATIVE: HOW TO GIVE FEEDBACK AND DIRECTION

awesome creative." While that's partially true, here's the problem: When a client pokes enough holes over enough time, they start to suspect that maybe you haven't been listening in your one-to-ones, and haven't learned their business as well as you promised you would. Then they trust you less, so they poke more holes, so they trust you even less because they feel like they have to poke more holes. Vicious cycle #1. Worse, when clients feel like they can't trust you, they start mandating solutions instead of asking you to solve problems. Which frustrates you and the team, which makes the relationship more tense, which leads to less trust. Vicious cycle #2. Also, less trust leads to worse work which leads right back to more holes. Now consider this:

When you're the one poking holes, you get to fix them.

Since you've invested so much time in the client relationship, you understand their business challenges, their pain points, and their anxieties. You know what keeps them up at night. You can empathize with them. When the team brings in work that you anticipate the client won't buy, you can give them the chance to solve it in a way that keeps the idea intact or makes it even better. If they're unable to, then that's a reason to abandon the idea and pursue stronger creative approaches. Either way, your hole-poking gives the team a better understanding of the client's business. It contributes to their professional growth.

You don't have to make every change you think a client will ask for. There's a difference between solving their business problems and giving them everything they want. And no matter how well you know a client, you still never know exactly what they're going to want. And by the way, some of the things they want may not be what you want creatively, which counts for something. So when you see potential issues that might not be issues at all, point them out. But instead of always asking the team to fix them, ask them to be prepared to discuss with the client how they would fix it. This can be a good compromise—you'll still be prepared for the review with thoughtful answers, and you're in the clear if the client never trots out the pokin' stick. Plus, it's another opportunity for the team to learn how you think.

When you put on your client hat, it's not because you're the enemy of creativity. It's exactly the opposite. You want to give your team the opportunity to sell the most creative work. And to do that, you need to make it bulletproof. So when you share work with your clients you can point out the things you solved for them proactively. They trust you more. They poke less holes. You get license to solve their problems more and more creatively. You sell more work. Everybody wins.

To be a responsible creative leader, you also need to understand how to be a client.

Why #11: Because Somebody Very Important Said So

When you've invested time in building relationships with your clients, they're more likely to take your advice. But sometimes, a mandate comes from on high. If your client has a charismatic CEO that's at the center of their company's cult of personality, you can expect to get these mandates. They may be based on actual, real-time feedback. Or they may be based on an offhand comment the CEO has made in the past. That's because these CEO's have become so successful, and so inaccessible, that anything they say is cherished like a rare gem.

When I was at Apple, there was a particular color we weren't supposed to use. Legend had it that years before, Steve had mentioned in a review that he didn't like it. Never mind that the color in question was for a specific execution in a specific assignment. Or that he may have changed his mind in the intervening years. Or that he may not actually have said anything about that color at all. That opalescent pearl of information had been passed down and codified, and the color was forever verboten.

CHAPTER 7   CREATE CREATIVE: HOW TO GIVE FEEDBACK AND DIRECTION

When Apple launched the iPad, I was on the team that created the hero line. We came up with hundreds of options. Clever lines, funny lines, straightforward lines, serious lines, lines that changed the punctuation of common phrases. We wrote options about product features. We talked about how it unlocked creativity. And did we mention that you could buy a pretty case? After months of work, we showed our carefully crafted copy to Steve. Or, to be more precise, the one or two people who were allowed access to Steve's inner sanctum showed him the work. The rest of us waited for a decision on which of our lines would herald in a new age of mobile computing. Here's what came back:

"Steve said he wants the line to say A Magical And Revolutionary Product At An Unbelievable Price."

And so it was.

At Apple, Steve said so, and later Tim said so. And while I haven't worked for Sundar, Saatya, Jack, Mark, or Marc, I'm pretty sure that when they say so, there's not a whole lot of room for pushback. It's not the most helpful feedback to give your team, but at least it's never personal.

Sometimes why is just because.

Hey Kevin, Didn't You Say There Were 10 Whys?

I did indeed. Nice job asking a question before you jumped into feedback about how I need to change things! Thank you for paying attention.

CHAPTER 7   CREATE CREATIVE: HOW TO GIVE FEEDBACK AND DIRECTION

Very Funny. Do I Get To Give My Subjective Opinion Yet?

Almost. But first, I'd recommend asking the team one more question:

"What do you like?"

This may catch them by surprise. Chances are, they're used to their creative leaders marching in and playing Keep It/Kill it/Rip It Off The Wall And Mime Wiping Your Butt With It. But giving them a say in the process makes them feel empowered. It shows that you are open to their opinions and their feedback. Plus, after you've listened to the team's opinion and shared your own, if you like what they like, they feel validated, and will feel more confident in their future creative choices. If you don't like it, they still feel heard. It's win-win. And even if you don't like the ideas that they do, you can still offer them the opportunity to develop the ideas further. You can give them clear feedback why an idea is not working for you, and what they need to do to move it forward. Then you've empowered them to choose whether they want to pursue it further. It's win-win-win.

The Last Why: Because You Like It

You've asked thoughtful questions. You've given objective reasons why you think some approaches are working and others aren't. The team has addressed all of your feedback, and it's so solid that it crushes your finger when you try to poke a hole in it. Now, at last, you get to like blue better than green.

But when you do give subjective feedback, I recommend saying something like this:

"Thank you for being so thorough with your work. Because you've made it all so objectively bulletproof, now I have the luxury of being subjective."

It shows the team that you value their effort and business sense as much as their creativity. It acknowledges that your opinion is just that, and not the immutable truth. And it shows that you understand that sharing your perspective isn't your god-given right as a creative leader. It's a gift from the team, and you are grateful. But even subjective feedback can be a learning opportunity for your team. Your taste is one reason you were put in a leadership role. Sharing your personal opinions, and why you hold them, is valuable information for the team as they develop their own styles.

Sharing your taste doesn't just have to happen in creative reviews. It *shouldn't* just happen in creative reviews. When you see a piece of work in the trades, in the award shows, or on your way into the office, share it with the team. Tell them what you think worked about it and didn't. You can even set up regular time with the team to talk through work that's out there in the industry that you want to critique, copy, or steal. Judging outside work is a way to let your team learn your tastes without any emotional downside for them. It gives them an opportunity to share their opinions. And it shows them that you are just as passionate about creative as they are.

One last note on giving your opinion—just like you pick your battles with your clients, pick them with the team. Ask yourself if you're making an important change, or just marking your territory. Does your subjective feedback make the idea better, or just different? Another way to think about it is whether it's more important that you get the shade of green that you want, or that you empower the team to make the call.

I know which one I choose most of the time.

Why #1 Redux: It Made You Feel Something

You've given every wrinkle of your left brain time to speak its mind. Now give the work one last gut check. Reflect on how it made you feel at the very beginning, before you approached it rationally. Do you still get those same tingles of emotion after giving your feedback, or did your direction dampen the blow? Are there ideas you walked away from because they didn't tick all of the boxes, but are so sticky that you just can't stop thinking about them? Ideally, all of the work will be both emotionally compelling and rationally bulletproof. But always pursue the idea that makes you feel something.

Remember, lead with your heart first. And last.

Making Decisions

Another reason that giving creative feedback is scary is that it means you have to make decisions. And fear of making the wrong decision is something that holds many leaders back. Well, you are going to make wrong decisions. Lots and lots of them. Hopefully you've created an environment that gives people room to be wrong, and as the CEO of your team, you've hired people who can help you be wrong less. But you'll still have to make a decision. Because the alternative is not making a decision at all, which will hold you back. Here are a few things that may make the decision process a little less scary.

When you're wrong, which will be a lot, you will generally have the opportunity to change your mind until the work is live. And even then, if you're really, really wrong (which you will also be from time to time), you can still go back to the edit room, or recode the site, or re-record a voiceover. And if you're wrong about something that you can't change, the good thing about advertising is that most of the time the creative decisions are inconsequential to the world at large. Finally, remember that statistically you only have to be right 51% of the time. Also, that is not an actual statistic based in actual research.

Now, set all of that aside for a moment. Because here's the key to freeing yourself from the fear of making a wrong decision:

Leaders are expected to be wrong.

Say what? Aren't leaders supposed to have all of the answers? That's why they're leaders. As it turns out, the exact opposite of what you've been taught your entire career is true. When you're wrong, you also get to show that you can learn from your mistakes, and make better decisions down the road. It gives you the opportunity to take responsibility for your actions. And your willingness to make wrong decisions sets an example for your team. When they have permission to be wrong, it leads to an environment where they feel safe to take creative risks and do better work.

When you give feedback, be confident. Be clear. Be decisive. And don't be afraid to be wrong.

It's OK To Get Back To People With Feedback (If You Have Time)

Creative leaders are expected to give feedback in the creative review. Thinking on the fly is a useful skill, especially when time can be in such short supply. Reacting in the moment is also a truer reflection of how consumers will experience the work. Our medium is meant to be experienced in real time—no one watches an ad, and then a day later recalls how thoroughly it touched on all of the key product benefits. They just react to how the work made them feel.

On the other hand, you're a creative leader, not the consumer. You need to become expert at letting your emotions guide your feedback, and also thinking through the work rationally. And sometimes that means you need a little extra time to digest it. It's normal for clients to have a day or two to get back to you with feedback, so it's totally reasonable for you to ask the same of your teams.

CHAPTER 7   CREATE CREATIVE: HOW TO GIVE FEEDBACK AND DIRECTION

I also like to give work the next-day test. When I wake up the morning after a creative review, I see which ideas stuck with me. Often, they're still the same ones I liked the day before. But sometimes, it's an idea I didn't respond to at first, or an idea that I didn't think would stick with me at all. We're in a business where we promise our clients memorable creative. Start by seeing if it's memorable for you.

However, you can't just ask for extra time on the spur of the moment. Your team are on a tight schedule, and your monkey wrench won't win you their friendship or respect. Instead, invest in relationships with your project managers. Work with them to build time into the schedule for a follow-up feedback session with the team. Clearly communicate the schedule to the team—not only when you'll be giving them feedback but also why it's helpful for you to have extra time (and that you're grateful that they're giving it you). And when you do have your follow-up, show them that the time they afforded you was well spent. When your feedback is more clear, concise, and thoughtful than it would have been off-the-cuff, it not only makes the work better, it makes their jobs easier.

Be Consistent

In every creative review, you explain why green makes so much sense for every project, why you love it so darned much, and generally why it is the overlord of all colors. Green is the best! The team learns this, and over time they learn to bring you only green work. You lavish them with praise, and approve their green ideas with only minimal changes. And, safe in the knowledge of how you'll give feedback, pretty soon the team is exploring shades of green that no one had ever imagined possible.

And then, one day, you tell them you want everything to be purple.

Consistency builds trust. So be consistent in your approach to giving feedback, and in the feedback itself. Your team will learn what to expect

CHAPTER 7   CREATE CREATIVE: HOW TO GIVE FEEDBACK AND DIRECTION

from you, which means they can be better prepared when they bring you work. Reviews become more streamlined. Everyone saves time and emotional energy. And most importantly, when they feel comfortable in their expectations, they'll feel safer taking creative risks.

Also I like blue.

The Radicchio Man (And Other Stories On The Importance Of Being Direct)

Back at one of my early agency jobs, I worked on a lottery account. In addition to their super-duper mega multizillions game that paid off in installments over several years, they also had a game where you could win a more modest prize but it paid out all at once. The brief was about how great it was to win a lump sum instead of having to wait to get it in little pieces. At our first creative review, my partner and I brought a bunch of ideas in to the CD which hit that brief. He just stared at the floor, shaking his head.

"It's like this," he said. "If you won a hundred million dollars, it would be life changing. But when you win a smaller amount, it makes your life better in smaller ways. So, like, instead of having to buy the regular lettuce you could afford the radicchio."

My partner and I looked at each other for an uncomfortable moment, and then I spoke up.

"Um, isn't this brief about getting paid all at once?"

"Yeah, but think about what you could do with that money if you got it all at once. You could buy the radicchio!"

"I'm not sure I get what radicchio has to do with it. But you want it in the spot?"

CHAPTER 7   CREATE CREATIVE: HOW TO GIVE FEEDBACK AND DIRECTION

"No, no, it's just sorta *like* getting to have radicchio instead of lettuce. But not that. I'm not trying to tell you what to do. I don't want to shut down your creativity. Just think about the radicchio."

So I did think about the radicchio (evidently, I am still thinking about it). And to be fair, focusing the idea on the benefits of having a little more money wasn't a bad approach. In subsequent reviews, we brought in all kinds of ideas about the small ways in which your life might be better if you won this lottery game. But I never wrote a script where someone wins the lottery and is over the moon to be able to buy radicchio instead of (ahem) garden-variety lettuce. Finally, the client presentation was looming and we were up against the final deadline.

"I really want to bring in a script with radicchio in it. Write that."

Oh.

All he ever wanted was that radicchio, and we wasted weeks of creative reviews because he never asked for it until the very end. He was just hoping we would see the genius of his indirect feedback and execute on it all by ourselves.

Don't get me wrong, I am a huge fan of examples and analogies as a tool for giving creative feedback. But when I give an example of something as a reference, here's what I say:

"I'd like to see something like (reference idea). Now, I know that when some creative directors say that they want to see something 'like' something else, what they really mean is they want to see exactly the thing they just described. But when I say that I want to see something like something else, I mean it. In fact, let me be even more clear. I don't want to see the exact thing I just described, and if you bring it in the next review I'll kill it. I promise that I'll tell you if I want you to bring me a specific execution."

CHAPTER 7   CREATE CREATIVE: HOW TO GIVE FEEDBACK AND DIRECTION

And I say that verbatim. Ask anyone who's ever worked for me.

Another common kind of indirect feedback is the phrase "here's what I would do." Whatiwoulddo-itis is endemic to the industry, and I had one creative director who had a case. And by the way, this is someone who made excellent creative choices, with none of that bitter radicchio taste. One time, we were in post-production, working on the music for a spot. At the first review, we played the track.

"I would make the music swell at about 20 seconds. Give it a big end."

Now, that's not unreasonable feedback. But the CD didn't actually ask me to change anything. He just said what he would do. And I liked the track the way it was—I thought that the change would make the spot over the top, and turn a bit of subtle humor into a banana peel. So at the next review, the track was the same.

"Hey, I thought I said I would try making the music bigger at the end."
"You did."
"So why didn't you change it?"
"Because you didn't ask me to."
"Yes I did."
"No you didn't."
"Yes I did."

You can see where this was headed.

It went on until he lost his cool, and his voice swelled as he instructed me to change the track. And while I learned what it meant when a creative director lays down a Here's What I Would Do, the damage was done—both to the spot and to our relationship. Maybe I should have known better. I certainly wish I had realized that "here's what I would do" meant "do this." And if I could do it over, I would have brought back both versions so he could hear his feedback, and why I didn't think it worked. But the point is, it shouldn't have been on me to figure it out what he wanted. And it's not

CHAPTER 7   CREATE CREATIVE: HOW TO GIVE FEEDBACK AND DIRECTION

incumbent on your team to decipher what you want. As a creative leader, it's on you to give clear direction.

Now, I'm not saying that you shouldn't ever give prescriptive feedback. Sometimes, you want to see a specific idea. When I've got something specific in mind, here's what I say (again, please feel free to fact-check with any of my former team).

"I'm going to give you feedback on some specific things I want to see in the next review. As you know, normally I try not to be prescriptive because I respect your creative abilities. But (we're short on time, the client has asked to see it, it will make for a more well-rounded presentation, I think my idea is best thing since sliced bread, etc.). If you have other ways to solve the problem I am open to them, but please bring back the specific changes I'm asking for."

At least that's what I would do.

That Darned Box

I know it might feel like I'm putting a lot of constraints on the creative process. That creatives will come up with better ideas when they're given the unrestricted freedom to create. That the box is too small. But clear feedback delivered clearly is part of building a culture that supports creativity.

Here's a riddle my daughter liked telling me when she was younger: you're sealed in a room with no doors and no windows. The only things in the room are a wooden table and a saw. How do you get out?

The answer is you saw the table in half. Then the two halves make a whole, and you leave through the hole.

The creative mind can think its way out of any box.

CHAPTER 8

Create Success: How To Sell Work (Or: The Myth Of The Dog And Pony Show)

Here's the classic approach to selling work: An agency gets briefed, then they hole up in their creative corner dreaming up brilliant stuff, then they come back to the client a few weeks later prepared to dazzle them in the Big Presentation. They bring professionally produced manifesto videos, inspirational music tracks, glossy printouts, and various other pyrotechnics and smoke machines. An hour later, it's over. Sometimes they leave high-fiving because they nailed it in one try. But more often, their shoulders are slumped because the client didn't buy every last idea. And here's why:

Selling work happens in the process, not the presentation.

The real way to get a client to say yes doesn't happen in a single meeting. It's in all of the actions you take leading up to that meeting. It's the time you invest in one-to-ones with your clients, learning how they think, understanding what challenges they're solving for, and sharing with them where you are in your creative process. It's creating a team culture that puts relationship building at its core, and hiring people who will help you reinforce that culture. It's giving detailed feedback on the work and the detailed reasons why you're giving that feedback. It's poking lots and lots of holes. And all of that happens before you share a single idea with the client. Yes, there's still going to be a formal presentation. But treat it like an annual review—make it another regular check-in in your ongoing one-to-ones with your client. There should be no surprises. The way to impress a client is through the relationship you build and how well you know their business, not the song and dance you bring to the presentation.

Having said that, *preparing* for a presentation is a very different thing from turning it into a spectacle. Thorough preparation demonstrates to a client just how well you've been listening in your conversations, how well you know their business, and how the work your team has created will solve their problems. It shows you give a damn. So leave the dogs and ponies at home. Your ducks, on the other hand, should be perfectly lined up.

Polish Your Deck

There's a difference between a dog and pony show and having a well-designed deck. Just like you take pride in crafting your work, take pride in crafting how you share it. Call out key strategy points clearly. Set up each idea in a single sentence. Choose key visuals that highlight the humor, drama, or richness of the presentation. Make sure each idea is presented in its best light. Kern the type. Don't clutter the page with dense explanations. Edit mercilessly.

Think about the order of the work. Revisit the story arc that you laid out in the feedback process. Make sure that it still takes the client on the same journey the customer will take. If you have multiple executions across multiple media, show how one leads to the next, and how they complement each other. If you know which clients will be in the presentation, remember that they're your target audience. If you have a nervous client, you may want to put the idea that will put them the most at ease first. If you have an analytical client, plan on walking them through the logic of each idea. If you've got one that's budget conscious, lead with the small hardworking ideas before you dive into the million dollar TV production.

Check that your deck shows up at its best across formats. Are you presenting on a screen or on boards? If you're making printouts, they should be clean, aligned, and easily readable from anywhere in the room. Check that the color is true if you're projecting on a screen. Are you sending a PDF or doing a physical leave-behind after the meeting? If so, you may want make an alternate version that spells out in more detail the things you spoke to.

If the creative is your art, the deck is the frame.

Practice

You've invested time building a strong client relationship. You know the brief. You know the work. Now you need to make sure your mastery of the subject comes across clearly and concisely in the meeting. And just because you left the canines and equines at home doesn't mean you can't bring your enthusiasm. So practice what you're going to say. Practice speaking clearly. Practice your dramatic pauses and your sweeping hand gestures. And then practice them again.

Practice on your own, and with your team. Give everyone a part to play in the presentation, and make sure they know what they're covering. Make sure there's no overlap. I've been in way too many presentations that go like this: The account person recaps the brief and sets up the strategy. Then the strategist recaps the brief and the strategy. Then the creative team recap the brief and the strategy. Then they share the work. You hear the phrase "As (name of person before me) just said" multiple times. Practice can kill those Just Saids. It makes your presentation more compelling, and saves valuable time.

And the time you have to present will always be shorter than you think. The client will be late. Or you'll be late (but you should never be late). Or the client decided to tell you all about their weekend. Or somebody's schedule moved. Or someone decided to join at the last minute and you need to catch them up. Or the technology didn't work. So give everyone a time limit to say their piece. Set a timer when you practice, and hold people to it. If you don't, they'll run long. Make sure you have plenty of time to share the creative, and plenty of time for the client to shower you with praise. Or at least have a meaningful discussion about the work.

If you have access to the room where you'll be presenting, practice there. Decide where everyone will be sitting in advance, and have them practice in those seats. And make sure that whatever technology you're bringing to the presentation works. Ask the client to put you in touch with their IT person if it's an away game. There's nothing that kills the mood of a presentation faster than when your USB-C won't talk to the client's HDMI.

Practice until everything stops sounding scripted, and it comes out as naturally as if it were a conversation you had every day. You know your stuff. Practice lets everyone else know you know it too.

The Last Time/This Time/Next Time Paradigm

Everybody wants to feel listened to. And when clients feel listened to, they're more likely to listen to you. This is particularly important when you're recommending that they drop a few mil on Beardy, Official Mascot of Barbasol Shaving Cream. So start every meeting by proving what a good listener you are by using this phrase:

"Last time we talked about X. This time we'll show you how we addressed X."

If it's the very first creative presentation, then X is the key insight you all agreed to in the brief, or the initial directions you agreed to explore. If it's a follow-up meeting, X is any feedback on the ideas that will keep them moving forward. If you've moved into production, X can be casting, music, photography, or the user experience. X is whatever demonstrates that you are an active listener.

Then, at the end of every meeting, continue to show how carefully you are listening:

"This time, we talked about Y. Next time, we'll bring you solutions for Y."

This sets up a virtuous cycle of listening, because now you'll start the next meeting by saying "last time we talked about X..." only Y goes back to being X. I am also not an algebra teacher.

If any of that sounds familiar, it's the same format you're using for your one-to-ones. Because just like professional development, selling work is an ongoing process.

Don't Say How Cool You Think The Work Is

You've crafted your presentation until it shines and sings. You've thought through potential problems and pitfalls. Now the team steps up to present their killer work. And here's how they kick it off:

"This next idea is really cool."

There's nothing that raises a client's red flag faster than saying you think the work is cool. Now, that's not to say that the work shouldn't be cool. The team should think it's the coolest idea ever. And by all means tell your team how cool you think it is (and why) in the privacy of your own agency—they thrive on your praise and approval. But by now, it should come as no surprise that clients are looking to solve problems. They're looking to build brand equity. They're looking to sell product. If cool is on their priority list at all, it's because they're marketing their brand as cool, and not for its own sake. And if they don't think your priorities are the same as theirs, it makes it a whole lot harder to sell your ideas.

That's not to say you shouldn't be excited about the work. If you're not, it's not worth sharing. Let your excitement shine through. But instead of saying that the idea is cool, have the team talk about why it's smart. Have them describe how the work is dead on brief, and how it nails the consumer insight. How the ideas can scale across budgets and across media. Let them share their process, why they made their creative choices, their passion for their craft, and their vision for the project. When they wow the client not just with powerful creative but also with the smart thinking that went into the creative, it allows the client to come to their own conclusion about the work.

They may even tell you how cool they think it is.

Tell The Client What Feedback You Want

After you've presented your work, it's time for (yay!) client feedback. Now, I know that at this point in a presentation you are looking for approval, both literally and emotionally. And the natural next question to ask is this:

"So, what do you think?"

Resist the temptation. I'm not saying you shouldn't ask for feedback. But unless the client is already jumping out of their seats telling you the idea is approved, when you ask the question that particular way it's going to make the work a whole lot more difficult to sell. The reason is, when you ask people what they think, they'll tell you. You'll get high-level feedback on whether they like the ideas or not, micro feedback on the details of why you chose certain words or certain colors, and everything in between. You'll get conflicting opinions. The least experienced person in the room will feel like they have to say the most to prove their worth. Then everyone else will feel like they have to say more because they can't be shown up by the newbie. This all leads to more feedback than you will possibly be able to address. Which means that someone's feedback will be left out. Which means they'll think you didn't listen to them. Which means that they'll feel slighted by you. Which hurts the relationship. Which means you sell less work.

Instead of asking the client what they think, tell them the specific kinds of feedback you are looking for. Ask them to give feedback on whether the work hits the strategy. Get their input on whether the work is on brand. Discuss whether it communicates the key support points. Ask whether they see potential for the idea to scale across other lines of business at their company or across markets. Whether it aligns to their product roadmap. Steer the conversation to cover the things you've already thought through so carefully when you gave creative direction, and stay open to the points you might have missed.

You'll also notice that all the feedback I'm suggesting you ask for is objective. You're not asking the client if they like the work, or if they think it's funny, or if they would prefer a different shade of green. One of the most consistent sources of tension I've seen between agencies and clients is that agencies feel like they should be trusted to make creative decisions. And that's understandable. It's our job. But when we ask our clients to give us subjective feedback, it's reasonable that they would give it to us. When we ask for objective feedback, it gives us room to be the experts on creativity.

However, it's a two-way street. If we expect clients to let us make subjective creative calls, then we have to listen to their objective strategic feedback. So when they say the work isn't on strategy or on brand, or there's some other business reason that we weren't aware of, we need to accept that they know better than we do. If we want them to let us do what we are best at, then it's our obligation to let them do what they are best at.

Of course, the client needs to approve a direction at some point. Some clients have the confidence and experience to make decisions. But for those who don't, it's still best to stay away from open-ended questions like "what do you think?" Instead, take a peas-and-carrots approach. For those of you who don't have kids, here's how it works: your kid needs to eat vegetables. But your kid doesn't want to eat vegetables. Vegetables suck. On the other hand, kids love to feel like they have control over their own decisions. So, instead of saying "eat your vegetables" (only possible kid answer: NO NO NO!!!!! followed by throwing of vegetables across the room), you ask "would you like peas or carrots?" This gives the child power over their own nutritious destiny, and sometimes even works (I am also not a child psychologist). So if you're struggling to get approval, phrase the question like this:

"Which of these ideas are you most excited about moving forward with?"

Then you can ask specifically what makes them excited about those ideas. Even if they don't approve them right then and there, you can learn more about what will help you be more successful in the next round, and keep the work moving forward instead of sending you back to the drawing board. It sets up last time/this time for the next time.

What To Do When A Client Gives You Feedback You Don't Agree With

First, don't argue. Ever. I know you're passionate about the work. I know you want to defend the creative choices that your team has made. But the client's natural reaction to you arguing your case is that they dig their heels in harder, then you dig your heels in harder, and pretty soon everyone's knee deep in dirt. Worse, you could get labeled as Defensive or Hard To Work With. These are labels that, despite not having much substance, tend to stick to your reputation like gum in your hair.

Instead of arguing your point of view, seek to understand the client's. Ask questions. Remember the questions game? Exactly. Your goal is to understand why the client is giving you that feedback. Is there a specific business problem they're trying to solve? Has there been a shift in the market? Is there a new product update? Has their boss been riding them? Do they like yellow better than green? Also, encourage the client to ask you questions, so they understand how you arrived at the work without labeling you as the D Word. Once you have a better understanding of each other, you're in a better position to work on a solution together.

There's a special subset of feedback when a client asks for a specific creative execution. They see a problem, and jump straight to a creative solution. Try not to take this as an affront to your creativity or your expertise. Chances are, the client is just trying to help and not scheming to eat your prehistoric reptilian brain. But regardless of the reasons behind the feedback, your job is still to figure out the problem the client is trying to solve. Then get their permission for your team to solve that problem instead of them. I've sketched out two scenarios of how this could play out with an example you might find familiar.

Scenario A:

CLIENT: Make the logo bigger.

YOU: The logo is big enough.

(baleful stares)

Scenario B:

CLIENT: Make the logo bigger.

YOU: Can you help me understand why that's important?

CLIENT: Because I want to have more brand recognition.
-or-
Because it's on a billboard that people will be speeding by.
-or-
Because we're a national chain of opticians and our customers are nearsighted.

YOU: Thank you for that feedback, it's helpful. My opinion is that if we make the logo bigger, it will make the layout unbalanced. But I understand the problem you're trying to solve now, so let me go back to the team and we'll bring you some other ways to solve for it. How does that sound?

CLIENT: Aces, boss!

Also, I know that presentations often build in time for client feedback but don't leave time for you to have a meaningful conversation about that feedback. As a creative leader and CEO of your team, that's a process you can work to change. But when there's no time to discuss it in the meeting (or, let's be honest, the client's radicchio-laced feedback raises your blood pressure to the point where you don't have the presence of mind to ask why) say this:

"That's an interesting idea, let me think about it."

Practice those words, they are your These Are Not The Droids You're Looking For. Chant them as a mantra. Tattoo them to the insides of your eyelids. Write them on the doorposts of you house and on your gates. Then take a deep breath, and ask your questions in your follow-up meeting or one-to-one when cooler heads prevail.

Finally, no matter what feedback a client gives you, say thank you. Hopefully you've built relationships and had honest conversations long before the presentation, and you can genuinely mean it. But even if you don't, say it anyway.

Bring Back What The Client Asked For, But Also What You Want

There's an old saying around the creative business that you should never bring anything into the room that you don't want to sell. And you should 100% do that for your initial presentation. But sometimes the client will still ask you to bring back something specific, despite your best efforts to have them give you problems to solve and not solutions. In that case, you need to show them the thing they asked for. You need to make the logo bigger.

(a collective gasp of horror from the audience)

"But what about Wieden+Kennedy?" you protest. "They only bring in what they want, and never let the client tell them what to do." Yeah, I've heard those stories too. But even assuming they're true, you don't work at Wieden+Kennedy. I don't work at Wieden+Kennedy. And if you do work at Wieden+Kennedy, I hope you find the other parts of this book helpful. Also, nice job.

However, just because I'm saying you should bring back the thing the client asked for doesn't mean that's the only thing you should show them. You should also come back with alternatives that you think are better, along with a whole host of reasons why your ideas address the issue so elegantly. Even when the client didn't give you the problem to solve, you can still bring them solutions.

Here's the other reason you need to bring back what the client asked for: they remember stuff. It's not like they're going to forget that they asked you to make a change. It's exactly the opposite: clients who give that kind of directive feedback want to feel involved in the creative process, and their suggestion will be the first thing they're looking for. If they don't see it, they won't be open to anything else you bring in because they'll feel frustrated that you didn't listen. So show it to them. Then tell them it was such a good bit of feedback that it inspired you and your team to look at other ways to solve the same problem. Then show your better solutions. The client's happy because they feel like you listened to them and they're part of the creative process. Your team is happy because you represented their point of view. Or even better, because you sold their idea.

CHAPTER 8   CREATE SUCCESS: HOW TO SELL WORK

Think In Four Dimensions

As a creative, the most important thing was selling the single project that you were working on. The script, layout, edit, or code that sat two-dimensionally on your desk or screen. But when you're overseeing multiple projects as a creative leader, you also have to consider how to make the entire body of work the best it can be. You need to consider all the projects on all of your team's desks. You need to think three dimensionally. Maybe the event's directional signage is straightforward so the experience can take you someplace unexpected. Or the shelf-talker screams a little louder so the TV can be more subtle. A dry buy flow allows for a wetter splash page. And if you prefer metaphors to wordplay, hold on to your proverbial hats! Sometimes you need to sacrifice a pawn to win a queen. Sometimes you need to sacrifice a batter to advance the runner to scoring position. You need to decide which hill you want to die on. You need to pick your battles to win the war. To let a powerful idea live, sometimes you have to let something else die.

Finally, learn to make the work better over time. That's thinking four dimensionally. I am also not a theoretical physicist, but here's how it works: Wherever your clients are on the crappy to award-winning work spectrum, improve each subsequent project just a little. Bit by bit, replace the not-so-great stuff with stuff that's slightly better then slightly better again, until all of those slightly betters become good and then great. Turn the stuff that's already great into mind-blowingly great. The breakthrough work you do for the small, low-revenue generating clients helps them grow into large, big-spending clients. The cash cows who only wanted boring work catch wind that the creative you're doing for your other clients is working, and they want to dip their hooves

CHAPTER 8   CREATE SUCCESS: HOW TO SELL WORK

into the creative idea pool. Or they don't, but your other clients have grown enough that you can focus your attention there. None of this happens overnight. The transformation can take months, or years. But selling work is a long game. It's not a dog-and-pony show, it's eating an elephant.

CHAPTER 9

Create Gratitude (Part 2): How To Say Thank You

Over the course of this book, I may have mentioned the importance of saying thank you (and meaning it) in one-to-ones, the hiring process, giving and getting creative feedback, culture building, and at pretty much every other conceivable opportunity. But it turns out that some ways of saying thank you are more effective than others.

Before we get into that, a little helpful context: as you know, I am not an engineer, an anthropologist, an evolutionary biologist, a DEI expert, a data scientist, an algebra teacher, a theoretical physicist, an employee of Wieden+Kennedy, or someone who is any good at making charts or graphs. But I *was* a psychology major in college. And as a degreed psychologist (or at least someone who sort of remembers Psych 101) I will now do my best to explain the concept of positive reinforcement.

Positive reinforcement (or, more accurately, operant conditioning) is credited to a psychologist named B.F. Skinner.[1] B.F. wanted to better understand how living things, and more specifically human beings, learned. His theory was that your behaviors are caused by your

---

[1] Skinner, B. F. (1948). 'Superstition' in the pigeon. *Journal of Experimental Psychology*, 38(2), 168–172.

CHAPTER 9   CREATE GRATITUDE (PART 2): HOW TO SAY THANK YOU

environment, and how you learned those behaviors was based on how you were rewarded for them. Positive reinforcement is basically the idea that you are more likely to learn behaviors that you are rewarded for.

To test this theory, Skinner put a pigeon in a box with a little peckable lever. (This, by the way, is called a Skinner Box. As a creative person I bet you could come up with a better name for it.) Anyway, there's a lot of stuff that a pigeon in a box can do that comes more naturally than pecking a lever — it can walk around, it can try to flap its wings, it can say "coo!", it can cock its head as if pondering the mysteries of the universe, it can poop. But eventually, whether by chance or intent, that pigeon may peck at that little lever. And when it does, the Pigeon Gods descend from on high in a beam of golden light and deliver one shining pellet of delicious pigeon chow.

"Well, hey now," thinks the canny pigeon, "I wonder if I will be rewarded with ANOTHER delicious pellet if I peck that bar again." Lo and behold, another pellet is bestowed! So the pigeon pecks again. And again.

The pigeon has learned a new behavior through positive reinforcement.

There are variations on the positive reinforcement model that affect how fast behaviors are learned, how often behaviors are repeated, and how likely it is that a behavior will become a permanent addition to the pigeon's repertoire. For example, if the pigeon gets a pellet every single time it pecks the lever it may peck less often. It's learned that it can get a pellet whenever it wants, or that the reward becomes less appealing because it's so accessible, or because its cute little pigeon tummy is full. If a pigeon doesn't get a pellet often enough to reinforce the behavior, or stops getting pellets altogether, it's more likely to give up on lever-pecking. Typically, the most effective way to teach a behavior is to give rewards at random times that are not too far apart. The pigeon knows the pellet is coming, but stays curious enough to keep pecking for it.

CHAPTER 9   CREATE GRATITUDE (PART 2): HOW TO SAY THANK YOU

By the way, you can also punish the pigeon by giving it an electric shock when it doesn't peck the lever, or taunting it with insults like "A ruby-throated warbler could write a better ad than this!" Which as you can imagine, is not very effective.

While you are likely not training pigeons in boxes, if you have a dog, or a cat, or a child, chances are that you've used positive reinforcement before. And while the folks on your team are not pets (though they may occasionally act like children) the same principles apply.

As a creative leader, your approval means a lot to your team. And every time you say thank you, you are rewarding them. But, as our friend B.F. demonstrated, people are more likely to learn behaviors when the reward is closely linked to the behavior.

When you just say "thank you, good job," your team may not know what part of the job that they did was good. Did you think the art direction was good? The writing? The way they built the deck? The way they showed how the ideas worked across a variety of media? When you don't say thank you enough, or wait too long to say thank you, things get even more cloudy. "Hey, thanks for the work you did last week" isn't effective because so much time has passed. They've worked on a dozen other projects in the interim. There's a much weaker psychological connection between the behavior and the reward. And if you don't say thank you at all, there's no reward for the behavior. But by now, we both know you would never do that.

So every time you say thank you (which, by the way, should be a lot), thank your team for the specific behaviors you want to reinforce. Did they come back with yet *another* great solution after yet *another* round of client feedback? Say "Thank you for going back to the well on this one again and again" and reinforce persistence as a behavior you want to build in your team. Did they bring in a solution that no one expected? Thank them for being innovative to reinforce that behavior. If the layouts are beautifully crafted, thank them for their attention to detail. If they wrote 800 variations on the same headline, thank them for the thorough exploration. If they

CHAPTER 9   CREATE GRATITUDE (PART 2): HOW TO SAY THANK YOU

brought you proactive ideas, thank them for their initiative. If they nailed a presentation, thank them for the time they spent practicing to make it so tight.

Using specific thank yous to reward specific behaviors isn't just for the functional skills of their job. It's a way to help build emotional intelligence and the culture you want to reinforce on your team. Did they treat a teammate well? Say thank you for being supportive. Did they share something personal in your one-to-ones or with the team that might have been hard for them to talk about? Thank them for their bravery. Did they give you personal feedback that they knew would be hard for you to hear? Thank them for their honesty. Did they ask a lot of questions in a briefing or a client meeting? Thank them for their inquisitiveness. Did they bring you unexpected ways to help them reach their professional goals? Thank them for owning their career development.

There are ways to say thank you other than just saying it. You can have a team holiday party, host team events, create internal awards for the team, or invite the team out for drinks. But in each case, you can tie that reward back to the behavior you want to reinforce in your team. Make sure they know the holiday party is to celebrate the goals they've reached over the year, and in your sparkling holiday speech list the achievements that you are celebrating and explicitly thank them for the hard work they put in to get there. If you take the team out to play mini golf, frame it up as a 'mini celebration for a maximum effort on the project' (frame it up that way if you're me, anyway, and are unafraid to make bad puns. Otherwise use whatever language feels natural to you). Create internal awards for things like putting in the extra effort on a project, being a good teammate, or for winning awards if you're feeling meta. And when you take your team out for drinks, instead of telling them, "Let's go get sloppy!" tell them, "Thank you for working so hard on the latest campaign. Let's go get sloppy!"

One aspect of B.F.'s research that I haven't ever applied directly is the part about reinforcing behavior through random rewards—a person (or pigeon) will be more likely to exhibit a behavior when that someone

CHAPTER 9   CREATE GRATITUDE (PART 2): HOW TO SAY THANK YOU

(or somebird) knows a reward is coming, but doesn't know exactly when or how often a reward is coming. I'm sure this would work for a team, but as you know I give specific and rewarding thank yous as often as humanly possible. Creatives are starved for gratitude. They have graciously and professionally fielded feedback from clients, colleagues, and creative directors for their entire careers and *still* turned out great work, not only not receiving the celebration they deserve for their efforts, but often not getting any credit at all. So when it comes to hearing thank you, my theory is that a creative person's appetite is pretty much insatiable. But I'm not going to build a Frank Box to test that theory.

And while we're on the subject of conducting vaguely unethical experiments on humans, I want to go back to that thing I said at the beginning of the book about sharing what's in here with your teams. For this section in particular, it's not a stretch for your team to draw the conclusion that you are manipulating them using thank yous as a reward. And that makes sense; the whole point of B.F. Skinner's work is that learning is manipulation through rewards and punishments. But your team are not literally pigeons in a box, or rats in a maze, or hamsters on a wheel, even if there's a pretty good industry metaphor in there somewhere. To help your team avoid feeling manipulated, or worse, to feel that your thank yous are less genuine because they are being used as a reward, I'd encourage you to share everything in this chapter with them. Explain to them exactly how and why you are using positive reinforcement.

And then thank them for listening.

And thank *you* for plodding through that lengthy and more-than-likely inaccurate psychology lesson.

CHAPTER 10

Create Change: Your Creative Vision And Your Personal Brand

As a creative, your vision was to make the work great. You may have had a particular style that you envisioned, whether it was humorous, heartfelt, rational, or technical, but it always came back to how you wanted to express your creativity through your craft. As a creative leader, your vision needs to be bigger. Yes, you still want to make great creative. But everyone wants to do that. Your vision is your approach to making that creative. It's about how you are going to bring the work to life in a way that nobody has thought of before. It's identifying problems and opportunities in the creative process, and devising new approaches to solving them. It's asking yourself what would you change about the creative industry, and then envisioning a way to change it. You need be more than a leader of your team or your projects. You need to be a leader for your agency, your company, or the entire industry. As a creative leader, your job is to make your team more successful. But you can also make the industry more successful.

When you have a powerful creative vision, everyone is your team.

You know the visionaries who reinvented the way the creative world thinks. I may not have legal clearance to call them out by name, but

CHAPTER 10   CREATE CHANGE: YOUR CREATIVE VISION AND YOUR PERSONAL BRAND

I can call them out by impact. The ones who decided it was time for advertising to respect the consumer's intelligence. The ones who saw a place for women in a world of mad men, and room for people of color in the boardroom. The ones who saw a need to make design attainable, affordable, and comfortable. The ones who saw opportunities to be bold, modern, provocative, or truthful. The ones who embraced new technologies, but were not always subservient to them. The ones who ushered in a new day of warmth and emotion, or introduced a beefed-up approach to humor. The ones who imagined creative independence from media holding companies and just did it. The ones who thought ahead, thought small, or thought different.

Now it's your turn. What do you see in the industry that could be better? What are the things you wished existed at the agencies or companies where you worked? What kind of creative hasn't the world seen yet? People love to talk about how the ad industry is broken, as a creative leader you get to fix it. If you don't already have ideas, here's a quick list you could get started on: There is still a lack of diversity in advertising and marketing, and the lack of diversity leads to lack of creativity. CMO's are often MBA's, and we need more creatives as the decision-makers in the creative process. Traditional agencies and interactive agencies and in-house agencies haven't figured out a model to work together yet. Creatives are expected to lead teams when they get to a certain level, but what does a system look for creatives who don't want to lead and just want to create? Generational labels like Boomers, Millennials, Gen X, Y, and Z are a convenient way to group people together in a marketing brief, but broad assumptions about audiences can hinder creativity. How can data inform better creative instead of dictating it through formulaic best practices? How do we bring humor back to creative with data and best practices breathing down our necks? How can we give control to influencers and creators but still maintain creative integrity? How can creativity solve the ethical, environmental, and social problems the world is facing? And what, oh what shall we do about A freaking I?

CHAPTER 10   CREATE CHANGE: YOUR CREATIVE VISION AND YOUR PERSONAL BRAND

Your vision doesn't necessarily arrive in a flash of inspiration. There may not be burning bushes or pellet-bearing pigeon gods. Like all of the other elephants you've been eating, you can work your way up to a vision step by step. As a creative, you started by imagining the kind of work you wanted to make. As a CD, you can start with a vision about how you want to give feedback and guide your team to the work you imagine. If you run an account or a department, you can plan a new approach to managing them. If you lead an agency, you can envision how that approach will influence the industry. Your vision will evolve over time as your perspective widens.

You are still a creative. With experience, you can create change.

Creating A Personal Brand

When your breakthrough creative ideas are seen by the whole industry, it can influence the work everyone makes. When your visionary approach to creating ideas is seen, it helps everyone make better work. But before any of that can happen, you need to convince everyone that your vision is worth pursuing. You need to sell it. And, let's be honest, you need to sell yourself. You are the product. And that's why you create a personal brand.

Before we slip any further down this particular slope, let me say for the record that I am not a fan of the term personal brand. As you know, I am doing my very best to avoid clichés, jargon, and other consultantspeak. And I know that personal brand is right up there with corporate chestnuts like synergy, ecosystem, empower, and paradigm shift. So I'll ask that you try to not let a little buzzword like Personal Brand trigger your red flags and make it challenging to optimize for a bit of thought leadership. And I'll make you two promises:

1. I'll throw in an extra spoonful of snark in this section to help the medicine go down.

2. I wouldn't ask you to do anything I wouldn't do myself, so I'll put my own personal brand under the microscope. You can consider the guinea pig my brand mascot.

I'm asking you to develop your personal brand because it will help you be a more successful leader. And I'm here to help you be more successful.

What Is A Personal Brand Anyway?

Before we answer that, let's take a step back: What is a brand? Many people think that marketing and brand are the same thing. But marketing is just one piece of the pie chart. A brand is Every Single Interaction that a consumer has with a company. It's the company's reputation. It's the culture. It's how the salespeople show up. It's the architecture at corporate HQ. It's the kinds of stores where you find the brand, how it's packaged and what shelf it's on. It's whether the website is easy to use or mocks you with snide pop-up windows. It's whether you get a real person when you call customer service, or feel like a cat up a phone tree. It's the music that plays when you're on hold. It's the barista who spells your name right on a coffee cup. It's a patent pending pizza box. And, lest we forget, the product is the embodiment of a brand. A customer may never see the marketing, but sooner or later they're going to have to come in contact with the product if they're going to buy it. A brand is the tangible expression of a company's vision and their values. A brand is where the rubber of a company's beliefs meets the road of reality.

Brands need to be consistent. They need to walk the same talk day after day, decade after decade. You can't be a faceless telecommunications conglomerate one day and a caring partner in staying connected to your friends and family the next. Rebrands sometimes work, but they're expensive, and need time to take hold. And lack of brand consistency leaves consumers confused. Or worse, it erodes their trust. A rebranded company is a pointy-toothed creature or polka-dotted mushroom that is not to be trusted until the consumer learns more, and that can take more time than companies have to spare.

And by the way, one reason that companies need to rebrand is because they come up with the product first and the marketing second. Inventors are good at inventing things. But the most successful inventors are good at inventing brands at the same time as the product. Edison didn't just invent the lightbulb, he created a brand of innovation. Steve made sure that a thousand songs fit in your pocket. Og invent wheel and invention concept too! If you start by unifying your product, your marketing, and your values into a brand from day one, it's less likely that you'll have to rebrand.

Just like the brands you work on, your personal brand is every interaction you have with your colleagues and coworkers and clients. It's not just your work or your creativity. That's your product, not your whole brand. It's part of the bigger picture, but it doesn't cover every pixel. Your brand is the real-world manifestation of your creative vision. It's the culture you build and the people you hire to make the creative. It's the example you set. It's how you want the world to see you, and how you act in the world. It's doing it all consistently to build trust. None of it happens randomly. It's intentional. And you can create your personal brand the same way you create brands for your clients.

Tell The Truth

There are a lot of books out there on how to build brands (this is not one of them, duh), written by people who are better at brand building than I am. One common aspect of these books is that they introduce complex and frequently geometric models in an attempt to codify the process: the Pyramid of Marketing, the Funnel of Fun, the Venn diagram of Veracity, the Hexagon of Happiness, the Cuboctahedron of Customer Engagement. And as much as I would I *totally* love to see what you talented designers out there would dream up for the Tetrakaidecagon of Total Target Touchpoints, I'm going to stick with a simpler approach:

Start with the truth.

Telling the truth is the foundation of all great brands. It's marketing 101. I used to teach an introduction to copywriting class, and before I let any student touch pen to their very first awful pun headline, I made them do an exercise in truth-telling. I'd take a quarter out of my pocket, and tell the class that we were going to pass it around the room and each say one true thing about the coin. Their initial reaction was "this is going to be easy" (although "how is this dude gonna help me get a job at Wieden+Kennedy?" was right up there). The first time around, the game was easy. The things the class said were physical, observable qualities. It's round. It's silver. It has a picture of George Washington on it. It's a quarter. The next few rounds would get more detailed. There are ridges on the side. There is a thin ring around the outside. It says quarter dollar on it. Then their thinking started to become more abstract. They included knowledge based on their previous experiences with other quarters. Some have mint marks, other don't. The back has different images on it depending on when it was produced. Quarters produced before 1964 were mostly silver, afterwards they were mostly copper. They brought up how a quarter interacts with its context, how it can jingle in your pocket or be arranged with other quarters in a neat paper roll. Things would start to become more conceptual. A quarter is worth 25 cents. It can't buy a game of pinball anymore but it can still buy a gumball. The front and the back are called heads and tails, and you can use it to make decisions. We got mathematical, and struggled to recall our elementary school lessons on how probability worked. We explored the philosophical questions

CHAPTER 10   CREATE CHANGE: YOUR CREATIVE VISION AND YOUR PERSONAL BRAND

the coin posed: E pluribus unum means "out of many, one," but was that appropriate for a country that felt so divided? Does "In god we trust" violate of the constitutional separation of church and state? And why is heads almost always a man's head? We got personal, and shared stories of saving up our quarters to buy that thing our childhood selves couldn't live without or searching through piles of coins to add a missing state to our collection.

What started as a simple task quickly filled the entire hour. It probably could have filled the entire semester. The point was not to find any single truth about the quarter, but to find as many things as possible that were true. To train those budding creative brains to consider a problem from all angles. And from there we could identify which truths felt the most resonant, the most relevant, the most surprising, or the most unique.

It's probably been a while since you examined yourself so closely. Many of us never have. You know your name, your gender, your height, weight, and eye color. You know where you're from, where you live, and what you do for work. You probably have a handle on your personality traits, your religious beliefs, your political leanings, which direction your moral compass points, and your outlook on life. As you start to create the foundation of your personal brand, dig deeper. Reexamine the things you've always held to be true about yourself, and see if they still are. Question old truths that have evolved, discover new ones that have sprung up, and determine things you'd like to be true in a future version of you.

What are your strengths? What are you really good at? Which of those strengths align to what you love to do? Which of them align to your creativity? What makes you different from other creatives? What makes you different from other creative leaders? What are your opportunities to grow? Where would you like to grow? What are your blind spots? Does how you see yourself match with how others see you? What would you change about yourself? What would you change about the world? What would make you happy? What do you believe? Ask people you trust what they think is true about you, and see how they respond to the things you believe to be true about yourself. Take your time. Maybe even an entire semester. Reflect on which ones feel the most resonant, the most relevant, the most surprising, or the most unique. Find your truths.

Tell Your Story

Welcome back from your journey of self-discovery! I hope you reached enlightenment. Or at least got a good list of truths going. You've worked on enough brands by now to know how difficult it can be to distill all of the things they could say about themselves to the ones they should say. The same goes for your personal brand. An approach I've found helpful is to try to craft a story around the truth or truths that feel most resonant (this is what I might call a Brand Narrative if I were employing a proprietary shape-based framework. But since I'm just telling the truth, I'm sticking with a story). Great brands all have origin stories: the inventor who founds the empire with their last dollar, the ousted exec who returns to save the company, the coder who creates the world's biggest tech operation in their basement, the ragtag bunch of misfits who win the big game, or the mouse who becomes a steamboat captain.

Luckily, we are all storytellers. Since you've got a lot of truths, you may have to try a lot of stories before one feels right. And it doesn't have to be in words. I'm a writer, so I write. But you could create a poster, a book cover, a typeface, a sculpture, a film, a play, or a ten-second social media clip. The medium that your story lives in can be as much an expression of your truth as the truths themselves. Your execution should reflect your ideas. And like your personal brand, your story can evolve over time. But your core truths should stay consistent.

Here's my origin story:

> How I Broke Into The Business
>
> By Kevin Frank

CHAPTER 10 CREATE CHANGE: YOUR CREATIVE VISION AND YOUR PERSONAL BRAND

I didn't always know I wanted to be a creative. I was pre-med in college. As far as I knew at the time, the things you could be when you grew up were a doctor, a lawyer, or a businessperson. That's what everyone else at school wanted to be, anyway. And since I thought doctors made the most money (and I wasn't even sure what a businessperson was), that's what I decided to be. I slogged through the biology, organic chemistry, physics, and math prerequisites all the way through taking the MCAT. But when it came time to actually start filling out med school applications, I paused.

Instead, I decided to take a year off and move to Colorado, where I got a job as a ski instructor. Yes, I realize how fortunate I was to be able to do that. And that's when I realized I could get paid to do something I loved. Now, I'm sure I would have been a competent doctor. But I wouldn't wake up every morning and go, "Awesome! I get to be a doctor today!" I remember coming home for the summer after freshman year, and comparing notes with a friend. He had discovered that he loved biology, and lit up when he described the various creatures he had dissected. He's since become a successful radiologist, and I bet he still gets out of bed every morning content that he gets to pursue his passion. As much as I loved being a ski instructor, I knew I didn't want to do it forever. So the question was what else did I love to do, and how could I make a living doing it?

Well, I had always been good at creative writing. And more than that, I had loved it all the way back to elementary school where I'd script class skits. I could make people laugh. I knew I was better at writing in short, punchy bursts than long form. Plus, I was never allowed a lot of TV as a kid, which made that forbidden fruit all the more tempting.

You know where this was headed.

After I realized that advertising was my calling, I focused everything I had on breaking in. I read books on how to put together a portfolio, studied awards show annuals and trade magazines, knocked on doors until my

CHAPTER 10   CREATE CHANGE: YOUR CREATIVE VISION AND YOUR PERSONAL BRAND

knuckles were bloody, and showed my work to anyone with a creative title who was willing to look at it. One of those people was a recruiter at Leo Burnett. He looked at my portfolio, and then grabbed one next to his chair (people had actual physical portfolios at the time). "You have good ideas," he said, "but look at the level of execution of your competition." The spec work in that book was as polished as any real ad coming out of any agency. It turned out that a school dedicated to helping aspiring creatives put together professional-grade portfolios had recently opened in Atlanta, and those were the juniors everyone wanted. Just a few years earlier, my clever headlines scribbled above a product shot I clipped from the newspaper might have been enough to get me hired. But now they just made me look like the amateur I was.

So I applied to that portfolio school. And I got in. And a few weeks before I was supposed to pack up and move down south, I saw a classified ad in the back of one of those trade magazines I was still devotedly reading. It was from an agency looking for a junior writer. Now, let's be clear: Wieden+Kennedy does not put up help wanted signs for talent. But it was an agency, and I couldn't get hired anywhere else. And I figured real-world experience was more valuable than more time at school. So I applied there too.

Three years after I first decided to follow my passion for writing, I got my first job as a junior copywriter. And ad by ad, job by job, bite by bite I've been eating that delicious elephant ever since.

The End

So, what are my truths from that story? I'm passionate about creative and I love what I do. I'm willing to break away from the herd. I consider my big decisions carefully, and I make hard choices when they're the right ones. I like to teach. I'm a writer at my core, and even a funny

CHAPTER 10   CREATE CHANGE: YOUR CREATIVE VISION AND YOUR PERSONAL BRAND

one on occasion. I'm methodical and persistent when I know what I want. It's a story I still tell, and those truths have all become part of my personal brand.

Fast forward a few decades to the present day. Here's my current story:

My Current Story

By Kevin Frank

In October 2022, I was leading the creative studio at LinkedIn. Over the past five and a half years, I had transformed the team from the proverbial ragtag bunch of misfits into a finely-tuned creative machine that won In-House Agency of the Year. It's one of the career achievements that I'm most proud of. But after nearly 15 years at big tech companies, I hit a wall. Even though I cared deeply about my team and doing breakthrough creative for the brand, I had been looking for roles at other companies. There were some great opportunities, but none of them felt exciting to me. Nothing made me say, "Awesome! That's what I want to do next!" I didn't know what I wanted, only that it wasn't what I was doing. So I walked away from LinkedIn without another job. I decided to take a pause.

I promised myself to not even think about work until the new year. And for those first few months, I didn't do much but surf, take my kid to school, and watch every single world cup match. But then a funny thing started to happen. I had spent my entire career so focused on a single path from writer to senior writer to ACD to CD to ECD that until that point I said no to just about everything that might take me off that trajectory. But without the noise of the daily grind, I was able to listen in a whole new way. I became open to new things. When other opportunities came along, I was able to say, "yeah, I could try that."

The first big thing I said yes to was moving to France. My wife and I both share a love of travel, and we had talked about living abroad from the beginning—during our honeymoon in Paris years before, I even met with Publicis to get a sense of what opportunities might be available down the road. So when my wife said, "Hey, you know that overseas thing we've always talked about? Now that you have time, you should look into that." I did. I explored where we might live, and all roads led back to Paris. I researched French schools for my non-French-speaking kid. What to do about visas. What the neighborhoods were like. I figured out what sites to use to find an apartment and how to rent an apartment with no credit history. How to get mobile service and Internet. What to do about health insurance. What to do about finances. Eight months later, we found ourselves on a plane to Paris for a two-year family adventure. Yes, I realize how fortunate I am to be able to do that.

The other big opportunity I was open to was when a partner in a San Francisco agency invited me to lunch shortly after I left LinkedIn. First, he asked if I'd be interested in working together. But that's not the opportunity I'm talking about. At any other point in my career, I would have jumped at the chance. They were a respected creative agency, and he wanted me to bring in the leadership and management skills that I had learned client-side. But I wasn't ready yet. Besides, I had made myself a promise to wait before going back to work, and I had darned well better keep it. Then he told me that if I didn't want to come work with him, I should write a book on leading creative teams. He wished there was some kind of leadership guide for creatives, since no one told them what to do when they became creative directors. I also wasn't ready to hear that idea quite yet, and shrugged it off. But a few months later, his voice was still in my head. And this time, I was able to listen.

You know where this was headed.

The End

The core truths in this story are the same as the first. I'm still passionate about creative. My love of teaching evolved into a love of leading teams. I'm still willing to make hard choices. I still value taking time away to think about big decisions. I'm still methodical and persistent when I've made a decision. I'm still a writer. There's one big new truth that I've added, the ability to be open to different kinds of opportunities.

And while I didn't tell all of the stories in between, you'd find the same core truths if I told you how I got my big break at Venables Bell, or why I joined Apple and LinkedIn. They're coming from the same place. From the same person. From the same voice.

From the same brand.

Write Yourself A Brief

Brands don't exist in a vacuum. And that includes personal brands. People need to be there to hear your tree fall. So when you've found your vision and your story, you need a plan to get them out in the world. You need a strategy. And luckily, you know how to write those too. If you have a format that your agency uses or that you like, feel free to use that. I prefer a simple one, called Get/Feel/Believe:

>Get (your target audience)

>Who feel (your insight about them)

>To believe (your vision)

Here's what that might look like for a brand we all know:

>**Get** people who want to exercise more

>**Who feel** worried they're not athletic enough

>**To believe** that everyone who does physical activity at any level is an athlete

Here's another one:

>**Get** women who buy beauty products

>**Who feel** they don't deserve beauty products because they don't fit traditional standards of beauty

CHAPTER 10   CREATE CHANGE: YOUR CREATIVE VISION AND YOUR PERSONAL BRAND

> **To believe** that bodies of all shapes, sizes, and colors are equally beautiful

And one more:

> **Get** people who use computers for work
>
> **Who feel** that computers are only for doing business at faceless corporations
>
> **To believe** that computers can be tools for personal expression and creativity

But we're not reverse engineering strategy for brands we admire. We're doing ours. So, flipping the camera back around, here's what mine might look like:

> **Get** creative people who are in charge of teams
>
> **Who feel** unprepared to lead
>
> **To believe** that they can learn leadership skills like they learned creative skills

Or another version:

> **Get** creative directors
>
> **Who feel** that their job is to give creative direction
>
> **To believe** that their job is to help their teams succeed

Or this one:

> **Get** creative people
>
> **Who feel** that management is for suits
>
> **To believe** that good leadership supports creativity

CHAPTER 10   CREATE CHANGE: YOUR CREATIVE VISION AND YOUR PERSONAL BRAND

Or:

Get creatives

Who feel an extra thirty bucks weighing down their wallets

To believe my book is a better use of their hard-earned dough than a couple of cocktails

Just kidding, you already bought my book. I'll buy you that cocktail sometime if you don't feel like it was money well spent. In the meantime, keep iterating on your personal brief just like you would a client brief. Poke holes in it, tweak it, and refine it until you've got one that's airtight, and more importantly, feels right. Because next you're going to have to execute on it.

Bringing Your Personal Brand To Life

Remember, your personal brand is every interaction you have with your coworkers, colleagues, and professional community. It's the real-world expression of the vision you imagined, the truths you uncovered, the narrative you crafted, and the brief you wrote. You've found the idea of you. Now, the execution needs to match the idea.

Your personality is part of your brand. Are you outgoing, introspective, intense, witty, or warm? Are you humble or a humble bragger? Are you sarcastic? Are you emotional? Are you confident? How you treat other people is part of your personal brand. Do you look out for the well-being of others? Are you a good listener? Are you supportive? Are you passionate? Are you an Expletive? (Please don't be an Expletive.) Your appearance matters. Styling yourself as a disheveled nutty professor communicates something different about your brand of creativity than sporting all black and chunky glasses. How you move through your workday is part of your brand. Do you give a rousing good morning to everyone, or hide out

CHAPTER 10   CREATE CHANGE: YOUR CREATIVE VISION AND YOUR PERSONAL BRAND

behind your desk until your caffeine levels are acceptable? Are you on time to meetings or make people wait for you? Do you always take the seat at the head of the table? Are you soft-spoken or the loudest voice in the room? What is your work ethic? Do you take a lunch break? Do you use your vacation days? Do you fly business or coach? Do you use inclusive language? Are you always the first to give feedback in reviews? And by the way, how you give feedback is part of your brand. Do you use we or I when you talk about who does the work? Are you a teacher? A deep thinker? A planner? A connector? An expert? A perfectionist? A communicator? An overcommunicator?

In addition to all of the ways you can execute on your personal brand, consider all of the places where you can express it. Create a personal media plan. Tailor it to the contexts that will best help you realize your vision, and give yourself the ability to scale up. The appearance of your workspace is part of your brand, whether that's a whole agency or just a cubicle. You can display your work or your awards, photos of your employees or of your family. Your environment can be as clean as your minimalist approach to design or messy like the mad genius you are. You can have spaces dedicated to helping creativity flow; pool tables, foosball tables, or birds' nests. You can paint your agency credo on the wall or cover it with street art. How you participate in the industry is part of your media plan. You can speak at conferences or judge awards shows. Host a podcast. Rant on social media. Write a newsletter. Write articles for trade publications. Heck, write an entire book if you're feeling crazy. Or just show up at work in a way that reflects your personal brand truth.

The people who can help amplify your brand are part of your media plan too. This can literally mean hiring a PR firm—brands hire them, and so can you. I've even known creatives who hire personal stylists. But beyond that, I'm talking about the people you already know. The existing relationships you need to lean on, and the new ones you need to build to enlist people to champion your ideas and your vision. They could be partners in your agency. Your employees. Your coworkers. Your clients.

Your managers. Your mentors. Who will give your personal brand word-of mouth? Find your evangelists. Find the people who will wear your logo on a t-shirt.

And at the heart of it all, the work you're creating is the purest expression of your brand. Because your creative is your product.

My Creative Vision

When I started at Apple, I thought I was going to dazzle them with my creativity and teach them about great ideas. I was very, very wrong. It turned out that one of the most valuable brands in the world knew a little more about marketing than I did. But after investing many months learning the culture of the company and the marketing team, I started to see something that I could improve. But I started small, with just our team. We had a design-led culture, and the designers were largely responsible for coming up with the ideas. Then they slid them under the writers' proverbial doors with a note to "put a headline on it." This was the polar opposite of my experience at agencies, where writers and art directors came up with the ideas and the designers were treated as the manual labor who made things look pretty. So I envisioned a team where everyone could be conceptual, everyone valued design, everyone valued writing, and no one was treated like a Wrist. I encouraged designers and writers to work together on projects from the outset. I gave feedback on not just the writing but the design, and how they worked together for the overall concept. I listened to my partner and the design team when they had a different perspective. I brought on agency writers who could write great headlines, but who were also trained to think conceptually. I trained them to work with designers. I envisioned a team that worked in a more integrated way to make the work stronger. Over time, and with support from above and below, I was able to steer our evolution.

CHAPTER 10   CREATE CHANGE: YOUR CREATIVE VISION AND YOUR PERSONAL BRAND

At LinkedIn, I had the opportunity to build on what I had learned at Apple, and broaden my vision for what an in-house agency could be. I still believed that in-house teams could learn from agencies, but I had also learned the value of mission, culture, and leadership at Apple. I envisioned a team that could have the best of both worlds—I'd hire agency people who could bring the unbridled creativity of an agency, but let them create in a supportive environment. I'd build a place where people wanted to stay a long time because they felt taken care of, and not jump ship every 18 months because that was the only way to move up. A place where they could do work that was both meaningful and creatively satisfying, and take home a few awards while we were at it. I wanted to build not just the best in-house agency, but the best agency period.

As my story told, taking a break from the corporate world gave me space to refine my vision once again. And, as you might have guessed, I am now focused on sharing what I've learned about leadership over the years with a broader audience.

With you.

I brought more creativity to companies that valued management and leadership. Now I want to bring more management and leadership to the entire creative industry. I envision a world where there's no agency side or brand side or client side. There's just the side of creativity.

I want to help other creatives be better creative leaders. I want every one of us to live by the belief that our number one job is to help our teams be more successful. And that our other jobs are to be a therapist, a cheerleader, a champion, a guide, a listener, a mentor, a shield, and a sounding board. To build teams, culture, safe spaces, and teaching hospitals.

I want creative leaders to understand the value of creating relationships, and invest as much time connecting with our teams, our colleagues, our clients, and our bosses as we do crafting the work. That relationships built through consistent one-to-ones are the foundation for

CHAPTER 10   CREATE CHANGE: YOUR CREATIVE VISION AND YOUR PERSONAL BRAND

a culture that supports creativity. Relationships build trust. Relationships sell work, not dogs and ponies.

And while we're on the subject of selling work, I'd love to put in a request for an industry where we don't have to write manifesto-like objects anymore to sell our ideas or ourselves.

I want creative leaders to have the tools to give clear and actionable feedback. To explain, and overexplain the why behind our thinking. Why? Because when teams understand the reasons we're giving feedback, it sets them up to make better decisions themselves. I want us to have more questions than answers. I want us to leave our own damn opinions out of it until the work is bulletproof. And even then, sometimes it's better to go with the shade of green the team likes. I want us to become expert at responding to the work with both sides of our brains, and all of our hearts.

I imagine a world where our career paths don't have to end at CD or ECD or CCO, but can lead all the way to CMO. Creativity is the soul of marketing. Without creativity, marketing is just data and RTB's, and nobody wants to watch that at halftime. To get there, it will mean learning parts of the business that are outside of our comfort zones. It will take work. We may even have to make spreadsheets. While we're learning those skills, we can be the CEOs of our teams. We can hire people who complement our strengths and compensate for our weaknesses. We can trust them, delegate to them, and listen to them so we can make better decisions. Even if they're the wrong decisions. Which they will be sometimes.

I want to work in an industry where creative leaders are grateful for the work their teams put in every day.

I am still more passionate about making great creative than anything. My vision is a world where everyone understands the key to making great creative is great creative leadership.

CHAPTER 11

Create Connections: A Little Help From My Friends

One of the things I've learned about being a leader is that you don't have all of the answers. *I* don't have all the answers. And even when I do have answers, they're my answers. Someone else may have a completely different opinion. And it's my responsibility to take those opinions into consideration.

So I've asked some prominent creative leaders to share their thoughts on the subject. You'll find a lot of similarities with what I've talked about, and one of the things I've learned to do is pay attention when I hear the same thing from a lot of different people. But sometimes, their opinions will be different from mine. They may even be the complete opposite. But I wouldn't be doing my job if I didn't listen to their perspectives, and share them so you can make better decisions about the kind of leader you want to be. I wouldn't be walking the talk.

With that, and a profuse thank you to everyone who contributed, I'll hand over the mic.

***

CHAPTER 11 CREATE CONNECTIONS: A LITTLE HELP FROM MY FRIENDS

I think we spend too much time trying to define what leadership is. It's a futile exercise. The most important thing about leadership is that it's no one thing, it will shift over time. Leadership is not static. It's fluid.

PJ Pereira
Creative Chairman, Pereira O'Dell

***

Perfect is boring.

Margaret Johnson
Chief Creative Officer, Goodby, Silverstein & Partners

***

I wish someone had told me that the key to effective leadership isn't learning from past bosses. Or current bosses. It isn't Googling the title description and pretending to be something that you're not. Oddly, it isn't even letting the work define you. Or the latest 'Leadership' podcast. Simon Sinek. Or the latest '5 Tips To Being A Great Leader' list. Or being the last voice in meetings. Or the first voice on conference calls. That's all BS.

Here's what I've learned, the key to being a great leader is simple.

Be the leader that you wish you had.

Lead with integrity. Listen more than you speak. Take the team to lunch. Leave the party early. Celebrate wins.

Be the leader that you wish you had.

Geoff Edwards
Managing Partner, Creative
GALE

***

CHAPTER 11   CREATE CONNECTIONS: A LITTLE HELP FROM MY FRIENDS

I don't know of one good leader who has not gone through a brutal, brutal realization that they were not the leader they once thought. It's only at that point of transfiguration that you can become a real leader and learn how to put others before you.

I would argue that you cannot really be a leader until you have learned to give away credit for success to your team and clients and accept all failure as your own responsibility. Always.

Until you learn how to do that, you're posing.

Knowing nothing is daunting. But knowing everything is paralyzing. We understood that just making a start was the best thing we could do—because we also knew we just needed to get going, try stuff, accumulate mistakes, and a lot of them, fast.

You will, inevitably, bump into and trip all over the furniture. So learn to cherish your mistakes and honor where you tripped up. Pause when you look back at them. That's where you learn some serious stuff, even though you felt like s***.

Any kind of mastery is not gained from intellect. Mastery is not gained from talent. Mastery is not gained from ambition. Mastery is only gained from time and focus applied to your craft over many, many years. Do not conflate it with fame. Learn to accept compliments gracefully. Treat flatterers with deep suspicion. Listen (closely) to your complainers and cynics—not just because you might learn from them, but because they secretly care.

Failures are not always mistakes. It just might have been the best you could do at that point. Okay, fine. Apologize quickly. The real failure is to beat yourself up and not take the opportunity to learn.

Get back in the air.
And keep flying.

CHAPTER 11   CREATE CONNECTIONS: A LITTLE HELP FROM MY FRIENDS

Brian Collins
Co-Founder, COLLINS

***

Isn't it ironic that when we are really great at making great creative the reward is to become a creative director, doing less and less of what we love? Being promoted to creative director doesn't always mean someone is a good leader of people. And most CDs don't get professional training other than baptism by fire on the job. While some come to it instinctively, many learn what not to do from bad leaders and hopefully model great leaders who have inspired great work. Either way, it's important to tap into your authentic leadership style with confidence, grace and grit. Knowing you will make mistakes. Be self-aware and stay open to feedback.

As a servant leader, I believe creatives don't work for me, I work for them. It is my job to see their potential, help them do the best creative work of their career, help them grow.

It is my job to build a culture where creativity and innovation thrive. A culture of psychological safety and trust where diverse creatives feel free to play, to express themselves and their ideas. To show up as their authentic selves. Free to learn and grow. Free to swing big and fail without fear. We cannot be in creative flow if we're afraid. The brain goes into fight, flight or protect mode.

Fear is a killer of creativity and innovation.

It is my job to make sure the creative brief is inspiring, insightful and grounded in human truth. Making sure we're asking the right questions, solving the right problems. Making sure we have front end alignment with key stakeholders before anyone starts working. Making sure the team has the time and resources to deliver great work.

It is my job to know the business. Building relationships with clients, partners and stakeholders. Building business and commercial muscles and language in service to the business of creativity. Creativity that creates impact.

As a creative leader, I get my name on the work no matter what. It is my job to listen to creative ideas objectively and be open to the unexpected. Letting go of how I would personally solve a creative problem. Inviting diversity of thought. Getting out of the weeds. Letting go of doing the work.

We have to let go to grow.

It is my job to make sure the work is both great and on brief. And if not, it is my job to leave creatives with hope when they leave my office. Finding a nugget of an idea, a direction with promise or giving clear redirection. Rolling up my sleeves to help if teams are struggling. In collaboration, not in competition.

It is my job to give tough feedback. My personal approach is radical candor with kindness. We don't get better if we don't know better.

It is my job to protect great ideas and creative talent, as they make their way through the often grueling process of pitching, feedback, approvals and production. Helping sell great work and keep it sold. Helping build on the idea along the way. Taking feedback but shielding from too many opinions and seeing it through the gauntlet of thousands of decisions. Bringing my creative and production experience in service to the idea.

It is my job to celebrate wins, early and often. Giving credit where credit is due.

Helping creatives feel seen, valued and a sense of ownership. Trusting my creatives when they've got it and teaching them along the way when they don't.

And when an idea dies, as so many do, it is my job to both validate the grief and help creatives move on, building the resilience they need to succeed long term in this very subjective business of creativity. Learning not to take things personally.

CHAPTER 11 CREATE CONNECTIONS: A LITTLE HELP FROM MY FRIENDS

As a creative leader, I am a mentor, a sponsor, an ally, a teacher, a therapist, a cheerleader and a coach. Just not all at the same time.

As a practitioner and preacher of regenerative creativity and a big believer in the need to rest and recover to avoid creative burnout, it is my job to protect precious creative resources. Not allowing them to be mindlessly mined and left spent. Helping create more time and space to be more creative and innovative. Encouraging and modeling much needed pauses, breaks, balance and mental, physical and spiritual health.

As a hiring leader, I enforce a no jerks policy. Trust me, you'll know them when you see them.

Jean Batthany
Chief Creative Officer

***

Some tips 100% guaranteed to make you into a god.

"Experience is a tough teacher. It gives you the test first, and teaches you the lesson after." I'm hoping this will be a bit like stealing the test the night before.

First, know that you don't have to be a CD. If what you really love is creating the work and that's what makes you happy, keep doing that for as long as you can. Ask yourself if you really want to move to a leadership and management position and why. It's important to know thyself. Don't go chasing someone else's waterfall.

Another thing to consider before fast-stepping up that ladder, is that you have to have the body of work and reputation that leads people who work for you to believe you know what you're doing. So much of this is subjective. And as a leader, you will inevitably make the call that makes one of your creatives say, "what the f do they know?", maybe daily. Having a history of stellar work will tamp that down, at least to every other day.

CHAPTER 11   CREATE CONNECTIONS: A LITTLE HELP FROM MY FRIENDS

I assume you're reading this because the answer to the early question you asked yourself is "Hell yes, self" and you have a solid, if not stellar, body of work as a creative. So in no particular order here are a few things I have found helpful to know:

– There's time and place for a bit of ambiguity, but it's not at the end of a creative review. When teams leave a meeting with you they should know what to do next. Be clear as you can about what you like and what you didn't and "why."

– Creative feedback isn't personal, but it's really hard for it not to feel that way. It helps to get the teams talking. If you're not feeling the work, ask them what they like and why. Make it about the work. It's you and them vs the problem, not you vs them.

– "Allowing someone to be mediocre is the cruelest form of kind." — Anonymous

– As a leader, people look to you for how they should be reacting to certain things. They pick up on your vibe. Always try to keep that in mind. If you seem frazzled or frustrated or cynical, that will be reflected back at you by your teams. It's ok to feel it, but not helpful to show it.

– Excitement and engagement are better motivators than fear or discipline.

– Ego is the enemy*. It's no longer just about you. Create the space for your creatives to shine. Give them credit for their ideas. Give away your ideas, without expecting credit for them. Take the blame.

*Most everything I learned about being a Creative Director, I learned from the Stoics.

Greg Hahn
Co-Founder, CCO, Mischief

***

CHAPTER 11   CREATE CONNECTIONS: A LITTLE HELP FROM MY FRIENDS

Things that work for me:

1. **Team, Not Cult.** One person doesn't present all the work, one person doesn't have the loudest voice, one person doesn't get all the spotlight. A great leader lets others shine.

2. **No Politics.** Doing the work is challenging enough. Remove politics so we can be real, honest, and authentic, and focus on what truly matters—creative excellence.

3. **Build a safe space to create dangerous work.** You can't get to the right idea without a lot of wrong ideas. Create an environment where people can experiment and throw their weird-crazy-dumb ideas into the mix. Fear is the enemy.

4. **Don't forget to laugh.** Even when stuff is hard, find some humor. Life and work are too dry without it. When you hear laughter, follow it. It can lead to the most fun ideas.

5. **Finally, be decisive.**

   Linda Knight
   Chief Creative Officer

***

In any commercial creative endeavor, there's a world of ideas and a world of constraints. And great creative needs constraints.

But if creativity overwhelms the constraints, you get magical thinking where the creative doesn't perform. If the constraints overwhelm creativity, then you get creative services where the creative doesn't inspire.

CHAPTER 11   CREATE CONNECTIONS: A LITTLE HELP FROM MY FRIENDS

The most successful creative leaders learn to operate in the gray area between the two worlds.

If you're going to occupy that gray area, you need to raise the altitude of your thinking. You have to elevate the conversation on both sides. You need to understand the relationship between constraints and creativity, between emotions and rational thinking, and between the consumer's hearts and their minds. You need to help people understand the whole picture.

For that balance to work, you need to be in the C-suite or have the patronage of someone in the C-suite. Because if you don't, an organization where creativity isn't the norm won't accept it.

The most amazing people in the business look at constraints and see them as an opportunity to create something totally different, and not default to something that's worked in the past. Those people are rare.

But they're out there.

Hiroki Asai
Apple, Airbnb

***

A strategist friend of mine once told me: "advertising is the only business that writes its own obituary." It's fascinating how advertising—a creative business—struggles so much to embrace change. I believe that principles never change, practices change (one of my favorite John Hegarty quotes). I am listing below the principles I live by as a Creative Leader.

- **Give praise immediately**

    If you see something good, say something good. Creative beings are insecure by nature. We all are. A well-deserved compliment at the right time boosts confidence and increases morale.

CHAPTER 11   CREATE CONNECTIONS: A LITTLE HELP FROM MY FRIENDS

- **See merit in ideas you wouldn't come up with**

    This is the litmus test of a good Creative Leader. Otherwise, you'll create an army of mini "yous."

- **Don't gaslight**

    We are dealing with smart people. Tell the truth even when it's hard. Our industry has a tendency to infantilize creatives.

- **Know that nobody knows anything**

    It's liberating. Because what we do is so subjective. There are many ways to creatively solve a problem. Be wary of pundits preaching hard truths. Have strong opinions, loosely held.

- **Don't micromanage**

    Nothing is more demoralizing to a creative than having their boss redoing their work or hovering over their Google docs.

- **An idea is only great if it looks great**

    Never underestimate the power of Craft.

- **An idea always needs to be big, not necessarily the budget**

    Don't let money (or lack of it) get in the way. Sometimes having too much of it attracts unnecessary oversight and layers.

- **Doing good, is good business**

    That's the power of creativity.

CHAPTER 11   CREATE CONNECTIONS: A LITTLE HELP FROM MY FRIENDS

- **People are not against you; they are in favor of them**

  Understand what motivates people and you will unlock the best in them.

- **Pain is inevitable, suffering is optional**

  One of the main tasks of a Creative Leader is to provide an environment free of politics and bureaucracy.

- **Promote what you love instead of bashing what you hate**

  This will change your life.

- **Who wants it more**

  Passion will take you further than talent.

- **Be a believer**

  Cynicism is the poison for creativity, if you don't believe that an idea can change the world, you are in the wrong business.

- **Have fun**

  Never lose sight that we make a living out of creativity. If you cannot change your situation, you can always change your perspective.

Rafael Rizuto
Chief Creative Officer, North America, Ogilvy

***

3 Things That Took Me Way Too Long To Learn, But I'm Telling You Now So You Really Have No Excuse, Honey.

CHAPTER 11   CREATE CONNECTIONS: A LITTLE HELP FROM MY FRIENDS

1. **Don't confuse being creative with creative leadership.** The first is for you and the second is for others. Build the conditions for creativity for others, because truly, your time to crack all the puzzles is over. Great news: you get to teach others how to do it. If that doesn't sit well with you, go freelance or ask to revert back to being a creative. There's no shame. You only live once.

2. **The weird stuff in your head doesn't have to drive how you live.** Thoughts, feelings and emotional responses can be just as transient and unimportant as the birds chirping outside your house. You're insanely imaginative. That can be your greatest strength or your greatest weakness. Know which internal voices are worth listening to.

3. **"It's easier to just do it myself."** will keep you and others small. And it's short term thinking. Maybe right now, in the moment, it's easier. But what happens when you have to produce the work? Keep your team happy? Or justify the lack of diversity in your ideas??? In the long run, it's never easier to just do it yourself.

Jaime Robinson
Co-Founder, CCO, Joan

***

Beyond the Summit: Embracing the Journey and Redefining Success

I've had an incredible career journey, ascending to the top of many mountains. As I reflect on my career, I realize a common theme: I would work tirelessly, scale the corporate mountain, and reach the top time and

CHAPTER 11 CREATE CONNECTIONS: A LITTLE HELP FROM MY FRIENDS

time again. But once I reached the peak, the glory I expected was often replaced by disappointment, and I found myself asking, "Is this it?" Feeling dejected, I would descend and feel like I was being "knocked down." I blamed myself, thinking I should have done it better, faster, smarter. So, I would dust myself off, bandage the wounds, and "pull myself up by my bootstraps" to make the climb again. And again. I was the embodiment of what Einstein referred to as insanity: "doing the same thing over and over again, expecting a different result."

What I was experiencing all those years is what psychologist Tal Ben-Shahar coined as the arrival fallacy. Arrival fallacy refers to the mistaken belief that achieving a particular goal or reaching a specific milestone will bring lasting happiness and fulfillment. People often think that once they "arrive" at a desired point—whether it's a job promotion, a financial target, or any other significant achievement—they will be permanently happy. However, research shows that the happiness from such accomplishments is usually short-lived, and people quickly return to their baseline level of happiness.

My older sister recently shared wisdom and love that deeply touched my life. She is one of the most spiritual people I know, and my faith has grown through observing her walk with God. She imparted sage advice, and one thing she said that I will not forget anytime soon is, "Run your own race."

Comparison robs us of joy and depletes our motivation because everywhere we look, we see people achieving different results despite doing the same work. I had to embrace the reality that what used to be is no longer what it is today, and that change can be difficult to navigate.

I learned to adopt a different perspective which is that I am exactly where I am supposed to be "in this moment." Change is the only constant I know in this life, and it is often resisted. As children, my sister and I heard our Baba (the name we called our dad) say, "View the unknown as

CHAPTER 11   CREATE CONNECTIONS: A LITTLE HELP FROM MY FRIENDS

friendly." He repeated this until it became part of our souls, successfully preparing us for a life that would present situations requiring us to adapt and evolve. Having navigated through four industries, it is safe to say I have made peace with and learned how to embrace change. For me, resisting it is like trying to hold water in your hand—futile and counterproductive. Embracing change, however, allows you to flow with life's currents and find new paths forward.

"In this moment" is the key phrase because it reminds us that this too shall pass. Be like water as it runs down a stream and encounters a rock. To the naked eye, the water appears to stop, but it does not. It may change direction and move to the right, to the left, or even slow down, but it never stops.

I am a journey woman who, for 25 years, has shown up in a lot of unique places and spaces. I would never have imagined spending almost seven years in a manufacturing factory or becoming the CEO of a creative advertising agency. Today, God has had me in the wilderness for the past year and a half. He has humbled me, shown me grace, and poured wisdom into me. I decided to take the road less traveled, and it has made all the difference. I have also come to realize that, for me, success is in the climb, not reaching the top of the mountain, which was my belief for more than two decades.

With faith as small as a mustard seed, I know now that once I arrive, there will be no fallacy.

Amani Duncan
Founder, Grit & Glory Agency

***

Well, the first advice I'd give to new CD's is to think back to all the things that pissed you off working for some of your CD's in the past. We all remember. Being given vague direction. Or no direction; as in "I'll know it when I see it." Or pitting teams against each other on pretty much every creative project.

Also, I'd remind new CDs that their creatives *need* love and support. Because what we do as creatives is kinda scary. No one likes to suffer criticism, but there are many ways to critique a person's work, even reject it, without discouraging them. Again, think back to your favorite creative directors. You almost always left their office knowing what you had to do, And you had enough gas left in your tank to get there. Be hard on the work, as they say, but love and support your people.

Luke Sullivan
Author, *Hey Whipple, Squeeze This*

***

Leadership is putting your people ahead of yourself.

Cindy Gallop
Founder & CEO, MakeLoveNotPorn

***

I've sat in thousands of creative reviews.

Internals, check-ins, tissues, workshops, brainstorms, rounds 1-through-6. These meetings can be momentum-builders, rallying the team around the work, or they can be firing squads, leaving the work full of holes and close to death.

Often, it's my job to jump between the firing squad and the work.

That means filtering anything that doesn't make the work better, simplifying what's left, making sure it's actionable and that the team is motivated to do it.

Filter. Simplify. Actionable. Inspiring.

Filter the feedback through your own instincts. Does it make the work better? Feedback can be technically correct and smart but that doesn't always make the work exciting and fresh.

CHAPTER 11   CREATE CONNECTIONS: A LITTLE HELP FROM MY FRIENDS

Simplify it. Are all those moving parts really necessary? What's the red hot core of this thing? Everything else is probably just a distraction.

Make it actionable. Your team needs to know where they're going and how to get there and your creative direction is the map. Is it easy to read? Is it clear? Is it useful?

Make it inspiring. People will go into uncharted waters with you if they're fired up about what they might find.

Every creative leader needs time to find their own rhythm. So consider this advice a beat you can sample, remix and play in your own style. And if it helps just one more great idea get out into the world, great.

Oriel Davis-Lyons
CCO, Mother NY
Founder, One School

***

One of the best lessons I ever learned about leadership was actually from an old coach. He said, "Don't expect anything from someone you wouldn't do yourself." In this world, it meant not to tell someone to do like 100 weighted burpees, if you wouldn't do that yourself, or at least try. I think about this a lot with creative leadership. I don't ask people to do things I wouldn't do. I wouldn't do ten rounds of work without clear direction and objections. Hell, I wouldn't do one round. I wouldn't just write things I don't believe in. I wouldn't work with people I don't respect. Somehow when we start creative directing or leading people towards creative ideas, we make demands that we wouldn't accept if someone gave them to us. "I'll know it when I'll see it," is the most classic and my most hated example of this. In no way, is this the same as "lead by example" or to "lead by doing." It's not about taking the work from people or doing it for them. This is about setting a path that you would be inspired to take or follow.

CHAPTER 11   CREATE CONNECTIONS: A LITTLE HELP FROM MY FRIENDS

Adam Koppel
Creative Director, OpenAI

***

It's about the 3 C's: Competency, Consistency, and Care. So, why are these the three most underrated leadership traits? Let's unpack each one.

Competency

I read a great book, *An Astronaut's Guide to Life on Earth*, written by Colonel Chris Hadfield who's spent decades training as an astronaut and has logged nearly 4000 hours in space. What's the most important trait of an astronaut, who's orbiting the earth at 400km an hour? Well, it's someone who's trained and studied so much, they can be relied on to solve unexpected, life-threatening problems with calm thoughtfulness. They're competent.

Consistency

A leader who operates consistently enables the team to relax and focus on high leverage activity. That's because people know what to expect, which means they're not wasting precious energy guessing what's coming next. You see, consistency builds a culture of trust and sets clear expectations. As part of those expectations, folks are clear on their degrees of freedom, which then builds a culture of accountability.

Care

We have to care about our people. I think good leaders stay awake at night worrying about their people and wake up ideating ways to help their people feel recognized and seen. Damn straight it's personal. In fact, I'd say meaningful work relationships are downright intimate. Because, how else will we know that they have a sick parent at home or what truly motivates them?

CHAPTER 11 CREATE CONNECTIONS: A LITTLE HELP FROM MY FRIENDS

Every person is created differently, but we all deeply desire to feel understood… seen… valued. Oh, you say you do value them? Well, do your people know you value them? How might you make that abundantly clear? Here are a few of my own practices:

1. Whenever I stay at a hotel, I use the stationery to hand-write a note to someone who's making a difference. A small practice that takes little time but actually uses hotel stationery! And helps someone feel unexpectedly appreciated.

2. Every holiday, I select gifts and write thank you cards for my leaders' families. That's right—not for them, but for their spouses and kids. This is a way to say 'thank you' for all the time their loved one dedicates to work. It's something I learned from my former boss, Kenneth Macpherson.

3. WAT or "Walking around time" that's booked in my calendar. This is time set aside to just walk and talk with folks. It's important because if we don't intentionally set the time aside, it gets gobbled up by meetings and we may never set foot outside the office! BTW some of the best personal conversations happen during WAT.

Emily Chang
CEO, VML West

***

Historically, our industry often portrays leaders as superhumans, endowed with exceptional skills and intelligence, creating an aura of invincibility and, at times, arrogance. However, the post-COVID era calls for a new breed of leaders—those who are open to vulnerability, who don't claim to have all the answers, and who recognize that part of their role is to care for the mental health and well-being of their teams.

Throughout my over three decades as a marketing and business executive, one of the most underrated skills I've observed in leadership is the ability to build brands and teams rooted in kindness and tolerance. By embracing these values, leaders can foster more resilient, innovative, and connected organizations.

Isaac Mizrahi
CEO, Alma
Author, *Hispanic Market Power—America's Business Growth Engine*

***

My advice to aspiring leaders is, stop aspiring.

You work in advertising—if you're anything above average, you will receive far more promotions than you deserve—even (and maybe especially) if you never strive for them.

What you should aspire to do is simply be the best creative you can be. Learn how to see the world in ways that others don't. Figure out how to frame work in a way that makes groundbreaking ideas seem well-grounded. Become immune to the fears of risk and failure. Develop the patience and dedication that great craftsmanship requires. Understand that the better the idea, the more stubborn you can be. Remain dissatisfied enough to drive your passion but not so much that it makes you miserable. Work for ideas. Not clients, not agencies, not networks. Work for ideas.

The most talented people in this business would rather work for a great creative than a great politician.

Kevin Lynch
Founder, The Wrong Agency

***

CHAPTER 11   CREATE CONNECTIONS: A LITTLE HELP FROM MY FRIENDS

- Find joy in helping others succeed.

People who chase the CD title because they want the power, and want the job simply because they enjoy telling people what to do more than being told what to do, genuinely don't make good leaders. I've worked for a lot of those type of leaders. Heck, I was that kind of leader when I first started out. It's a skill you have to learn, but you also have to want to learn it. If you only want your ideas to win, and if you want to be the best, smartest person in the room, leadership probably isn't right for you. Leadership is knowing when to pull the best and brightest people in the room, learning how to inspire and guide them, and when to get the hell out of the way.

- Get excited about working with people you have nothing in common with.

Great creative leaders don't hire people like themselves; they seek out those who are radically different. Because diverse perspectives and experiences make for stronger creative solutions—and that's not just my opinion; it's a proven fact, backed by people much smarter than me. That's why I always push for the most diverse teams and actively seek feedback from those who challenge me and think differently. The real magic happens when you unleash the team's collective superpowers by inspiring and motivating those who bring something entirely unique to the table.

- Don't speak in buzzwords.

Be clear and transparent, and always have a strong POV rooted in your experience—whether it's giving feedback on the work, assessing team performance, setting expectations, or selling ideas to the client. Don't bother with buzzwords or trying to sound smart; people will see right through that. Just speak in human. And don't just say an idea isn't working or isn't big enough and leave it at that. Explain why it's not clicking for you. This gives the team the clarity they need to pivot, or better yet, it opens the door for them to push back and explain how they see it—because maybe it does work, you just don't see it because you're wired differently.

CHAPTER 11   CREATE CONNECTIONS: A LITTLE HELP FROM MY FRIENDS

- Make the team feel safe, or the ideas will.

Creativity isn't a science, and trying things that have never been done is scary. To create truly breakthrough work, you need to be brave—and that only happens when people can share their thoughts, POVs, and true selves without fear of criticism or judgment. The team needs to know they can fail without fearing for their jobs. Inspire them to take risks, and embrace failure as a necessary part of the process that leads to success.

- Give a damn without being a jerk.

To build a strong team that creates, sells, and buys big ideas, you have to build trust. That only comes when you truly love what you do and genuinely care about the people you do it with. So, share your passion, life, and challenges with the team, and take a real interest in the lives and goals of the people you work with!

Build the relationships and find the shared goals. Then, you can have the honest dialogue and hard conversations it takes to push each other toward what you all want to achieve—creating the best work of your lives while having a good life.

Kelly Roe
SVP, Creative Director, Leo Burnett

***

When it comes to leading an agency, I thought coming from a creative background would be a disadvantage I'd have to overcome. After all, what did I know about finance and account management. Turns out, after I got over my imposter syndrome, I learned the opposite was true. First of all, agency finances are basically arithmetic. Not calculus. If you have a strong CFO, they will tell you that as long as the top line is growing, everything else works itself out. It turns out that managing the creative department is the hardest part. Not because creatives are temperamental or disorganized. Because you never know when lightning will strike. If you

CHAPTER 11   CREATE CONNECTIONS: A LITTLE HELP FROM MY FRIENDS

ask how long it will take to come up with a great idea, you have no idea. Could be 1 second, 1 day or 1 month. So if you can manage the creative department, you can manage an agency.

Jim Lesser
Chief Brand Officer, ServiceNOW

***

IF YOU DON'T LEARN TO SELL GREAT WORK, NO ONE WILL KNOW YOUR NAME.

To consistently produce great work, you have to become as good at selling it as you are at coming up with it. Think of a creative director that everyone knows. They are no doubt creative, but there's no shortage of extremely creative CDs. The reason you know their name is because they have learned how to sell great work to clients.

So how do you fight for the work?

You don't.

I can count on one half of one hand the number of times I have resorted to fighting, or argument to sell great work to a client.

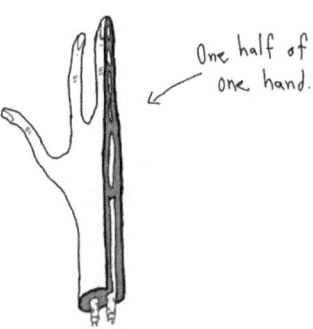

(I hope my drawing helps bring this difficult concept to life. I spent a lot of time on this—I think it turned out pretty good.)

CHAPTER 11   CREATE CONNECTIONS: A LITTLE HELP FROM MY FRIENDS

The reason I don't fight with clients is not because I'm a nice guy – it's because it doesn't work.

Because it's not you vs. the client. It's you & the client vs. the problem. You have to stop seeing the client as your enemy, and start seeing them as a partner.

That starts with understanding how most clients see you. Assume that the Starting Point of any new client relationship is that the client is suspicious and afraid.

They're afraid that you don't have the same goals as them—that you just want to make something creative and win awards, when what they need to keep their job is business results.

Even if you bother to learn and understand their goals, they're afraid you don't care about them.

They're afraid you're going to try to manipulate, pressure, or force them into work that serves your interest, not theirs. And they probably have good reasons for those fears. And unless you change those perceptions and fears about you, they will never buy great work. Because fear is the enemy of creativity. So we have to systematically eliminate, or at least reduce all those fears by proving to them that none of those preconceived notions about us are true.

Every action we take has to chip away at their paradigm of us.

We have to stop trying to "sell" the work to them. Instead we're going to eliminate their fears, gain their trust and respect, and let them know that they are ultimately in control.

Only when we have done all that will they be in a position to approve the amazing creative work that will help their business and brand, which happens to be exactly the kind of work that will catapult your career.

CHAPTER 11   CREATE CONNECTIONS: A LITTLE HELP FROM MY FRIENDS

Jason Bagley
Founder, The Audacious School of Astonishing Pursuits

***

Learn to speak the next step before you take it.

The first part of our career as a creative is learning the craft. We become experts at type, color, style, headlines—all aspects of design, writing, or video. And as our careers grow, we assume that the way to take that next leadership role is all about being even better at the craft. Being the most talented. Having the best portfolio or awards.

But that's naive. The reality is that as you become more of a leader, you have to learn a completely different set of skills. Less hard skills and more soft skills. You have to learn to build and maintain trusting relationships. You need a greater understanding of business and marketing strategy. You have to appreciate and navigate finance and operational challenges. The type of stuff you used to roll your eyes at and say, "That's something the account person or project manager will handle."

In fact, when executives at a company are looking for the next creative leader, they are judging you on a completely different set of criteria. They are looking for skills and leadership qualities that they understand and recognize. And they don't speak design or storytelling, necessarily.

So before you expect to have a seat at the table with a larger leadership role, understand that you have to learn to speak a handful of new languages. At the table, they may be speaking operations and finance. Your ability to discuss tasty kerning or white space may be irrelevant. They aren't going to give you leadership respect or a role, unless you can communicate toe to toe with them.

Which means, you have to become fluent in these new business languages. I've always said on Real Creative Leadership, that if you want to lead, you have to read. Read books on business strategy. Take a marketing strategy class at a local university or get a new degree. Watch videos or listen to podcasts on leadership. Do whatever you can to learn the language of the table where you want a seat.

Only then will you be seen as a capable leader. One they trust. One that will not only bring the brand to life and deliver amazing creative experiences, but who will understand how those fit into the greater business strategy.

Creative leadership is about building an environment where creativity can thrive. Where ideas have a chance to live. As a creative leader, it's your job to create those opportunities. And that means you need a seat at the leadership table, to influence decisions related to that environment. So start reading and studying—so you can speak the language of business.

Adam Morgan
VP of Brand, Twilio

***

I surprise myself every day with what I can still learn. Adopting a creative problem solving mindset keeps the world in a pretty interesting place. The everyday is juicy with information and inspiration. It's in the nooks and crannies of living. The trick is to not get stuck in your ways and keep your eyes open.

Tavia Holmes
Executive Creative Director, LinkedIn

***

Lead with conviction.

This approach isn't the only way, but plays an important role in the creative industry and is the difference between authentically rallying troops around a singular vision and going through the motions. The key is you must deeply believe in the mission. Leading with conviction also

CHAPTER 11   CREATE CONNECTIONS: A LITTLE HELP FROM MY FRIENDS

filters down through the work, and ultimately bleeds through in everything we make, say, do. It shows up in the output of the work and informs our strategy, messaging, tone, craft, execution, results. If we get this right, our conviction permeates throughout the business and culture writ large. Count yourself as fortunate if you get to be selective about the brands you build, businesses you work for and stories you craft—also take this as a great responsibility. As brand builders, we are the gatekeepers of culture and public sentiment, as such, be sure to be rigorous in the application of your conviction. If you do, it will guide you to good, meaningful and inspiring places.

>Cameron Ewing
>VP, Creative and Brand

***

I've been incredibly lucky in my career to have worked only* for companies that are, or were, inherently and famously creative—visionary, ambitious and principled. In those places, like Apple and Wieden+Kennedy and BBH (in its independent days), I'd argue that the geniuses behind those businesses weren't necessarily great leaders or managers, but they were uniquely great at creating environments where the creative bar was high, originality was expected, and talent and intuition were trusted. Failure was expected and okay, as long as you were right more often than you were wrong.

I've translated that learning, in my two decades of leading highly-functioning, highly-awarded creative teams, into a focus more on creating the right environment and the right level of expectations, than creating work itself.

Now, some creative leaders like to get their hands dirty and put those dirty fingerprints over other people's work, but not lazy ol' me.

CHAPTER 11   CREATE CONNECTIONS: A LITTLE HELP FROM MY FRIENDS

I like to hire carefully, instinctively (when I was a mid-level creative, John Butler of Butler, Shine and Stern once told me to always hire people better than you) and then give those folks the opportunity to do what they're good at.

So boring process thing: If something is making people worse at their jobs, do whatever it takes, ruffle some feathers, and change it.

And not boring thing: Make surprising yourselves and each other a priority and the most basic expectation. Team people up or cast projects in a way that allows for people to break muscle memory and genuinely surprise themselves with the crazy or crazily smart things that they come up with. At Apple, I ran an international team of creatives from more than 40 countries, for almost all of whom English was their second language. There were some amazing situations where small misunderstandings (a gap in cultural references, or a mistranslation in someone's head) led to creative solutions that were genius and well, surprising. Surprise is the antidote to sameness and mediocrity so making that the thing you chase, executed with a bit of intelligence and taste, creates work that will surprise people out there in the real world too.

And then, and this may be the most important thing I have to say, is that for the above to work, you have to get your teams to believe and believe that you believe. Bill Bernbach famously said (and I misquote): "A principle's not a principle unless it costs you something." So stick your neck out. Have some public failures yourself. Fire the client that's sucking you and your teams dry. Say no to the potential client who says they want to be "just like Apple" but will never be anything like Apple because they don't know that Bill Bernbach quote.

*I say I've only worked for creatively ambitious and principled places but a glance at my LinkedIn will show that's not entirely true.

CHAPTER 11   CREATE CONNECTIONS: A LITTLE HELP FROM MY FRIENDS

Dean Wei
Chief Creative Officer

***

You get this job because you love it, not because of how old you are or because of ego. Creative leadership is not about you anymore; it's about all the people you lead, it's about them and their careers. "Those who know, do. Those who understand, teach."—Plato

This job is about understanding and explaining The Why. Why did ideas die, why are ideas great? Because you know what you're talking about. When you share the why, now creative reviews and critiques can inspire. As a junior and mid I might have had all my ideas slaughtered but if I knew why, then I was excited to start again.

You have to be a student of this business. Know thy history, read thy current articles. Don't let your people work their butt off for a great idea… that's already been done.

You facilitate the spectacle of the accounts you lead. You're in charge of the account, projects, briefs, and people's enthusiasm.

Just because you're in charge of everything doesn't mean you do everything. Don't compete, inspire. But! You are the last line of defense should the timeline overrun your positions. If they can't crack it and it's all due a day from now, it's time to throw your ideas onto the wall.

It's fun to be in charge, right? Not all the time. You gotta do the hard stuff, too. Like letting people go. And this is hard stuff.

Create a safe space to fail. We all do. You have to understand that creative people are delicate flowers and broken toys.

Value diversity of thought. You don't need anyone who thinks like you.

Be honest. Tell the truth with clients, bosses, reports, teammates.

CHAPTER 11   CREATE CONNECTIONS: A LITTLE HELP FROM MY FRIENDS

See everyone as individuals. What makes them tick. Then lean into that.

Let people work where and when they work best. Clock-watching and bed checks are the last bastions of weak managers.

The glass is not half empty, nor is it also trying to kill you. Be a realist, but optimism rules the roost.

This business is not about loyalty. It's about creating a place where your people can make the best work of their careers. Make sure they are building their portfolio so they can leave anytime they want. Make them that good.

Remember, we're all in this alone. Life, work, anything is a team effort. But it's really not. Impact is the currency of business. Do you create impact?

We are naturally subversive people. But once you are gifted with titles of leadership you're the navy, not a pirate. The agency is not the enemy because you are now the agency.

Keep the Peace. Run at conflict: solve it soon. Be aware of partnerships that aren't working.

Squeeze your ECD/CCO. Get their POV, expectations, instincts at beginning, middle, end.

Very important: always make sure you believe you are working for someone who is better than you.

Be decisive. That's all the world wants from you. "Keep going" and "I'll know it when I see it" is a waste of everyone's time. Be a creative director, not a creative inspector.

Inspire prolific thinking. To hell with reductionism. Get people digging lots of quick holes.

CHAPTER 11   CREATE CONNECTIONS: A LITTLE HELP FROM MY FRIENDS

Teach your people the secret of staying in this business: be professional creatives. The creativity part is table stakes—you either are or aren't. It's being on time, and prolific. Always make more than was asked for. You do this, and you'll stay in the game as long as you want.

Talent is better than money. The more money you make the less time you'll stay employed. Be talented and you work forever.

On big assignments and pitches, stay calm. We jump off a cliff and make a parachute on the way down. You're never done, you just have a due date.

Prioritize what can be great, and what's a thing to get done quickly and professionally. And don't fight it. When eating a turd, don't nibble.

Not everything you work on is going to be great. We all have to sweep up after the elephants.

Know when to call in the big dogs, titles above you. This business keeps saying you should fight for your work but... you'll get asked off the biz when you fight too much—that's best left for high ups and other roles.

Hire weirdos and crazies. Beyond their body of work... the intangibles are important.

Know the importance of both idea and execution. They're both really hard, and different things.

Believe something about this business and why you're in it.

Tim Roan
Chief Creative Officer, McGarrah Jessee

***

What is really interesting to me about 'Leadership Qualities' is the fact that it is not a question that is truly often asked, however on the occasion it is, it is extraordinary how the subject is mostly evaluated by financial achievements, awards, press recognition, popularity, or simply the label of where one has worked. Is this leadership? Not to me it is not. I have always defined leadership by how much the humans around said leader are growing and evolving within their orbit, and even those beyond their orbit are experiencing the 'positive' aftershocks of effective leadership. This is the premier evaluation of one as a leader I believe. Secondarily, the ability to recognize and embrace your own strengths and weaknesses is another must have, gifted with the cognizance to hire those who complement such, openly and with humility. This creates what I call a 'positive domino effect,' connecting the dots and feeling the ability to empower each individual to be and feel valued, creating a sense of purpose within the ecosystem. Ultimately a superlative quality is the ability to empower.

Dany Lennon
Founder/CEO, The Creative Register Inc.

***

When it comes to making and defending work, don't be afraid to fail…or even get fired. While it may sound counterintuitive in a book on leadership, there's nothing more responsible you can do than stand up for work or thinking that you believe will result in greater success for your clients.

Jason Sperling
Chief Creative Officer, Innocean USA

***

Every job is broken. There is not a single job that I've ever taken that was not broken in the eyes of someone else. There is not a single job that I've ever been promoted into, left a company for or continued to stay in that someone said I shouldn't take, shouldn't stay in or shouldn't move hundreds of miles for.

CHAPTER 11   CREATE CONNECTIONS: A LITTLE HELP FROM MY FRIENDS

Looking back over the last 20 years, I've heard the term "broken" used to describe many roles I've stepped into: the company is a mess, the leaders are a mess, the company's best days are behind it, the team is too junior, the team is bitter, the team doesn't exist yet, the headcount is non-existent, the team had no credibility, the CEO is crazy, the president is crazy, the ACD is crazy, the future manager is crazy, the future manager is too good to be true (there must be a flaw in there!), the stock price is too low, the stock price is too high, the stock is too volatile, the company hasn't done any great creative work, the team hasn't won awards.... Oh, and my personal favorite, and perhaps the most damning label placed on by folks in our industry, "They don't understand great creative."

I've ignored most of it.

In a recent blog post, "Vision before Problems," one of my mentors, Rob Schwartz, wrote, *"Of course, the first thing a leader wants to do is tell me all the problems. But that can wait...No, I want to hear about the dream first. I want to see what you saw in your mind's eye that got you excited about this new post. I want to envision what you are imagining that's not there now."*

When I reflect back on all the people that I've worked with, there is a very simple dividing line: Those that spend their time focused on the problems around them and those that spend their time focused on the tremendous opportunity around them. It's the classic glass half-full, half-empty and it's that choice that separates the leaders from the pack.

In the day-to-day, you have to put blinders on. You literally have to ignore, block and delude yourself into thinking that the list of hundreds of broken things about the job you are in don't exist. For a minute. That's the trick. And you have to focus on the one thing you can control: the work. And if you think about it, as creatives, that's the one thing we're actually good at.

CHAPTER 11   CREATE CONNECTIONS: A LITTLE HELP FROM MY FRIENDS

When the work gets good, everything else tends to fall into place. And I've seen it time and time again. I remember a leader at Chiat used to say "One great campaign can change an entire agency." And it was true. The whole building swelled with pride when Apple's Mac vs. PC campaign came out. Or Gatorade triumphed at Cannes with Replay. Suddenly the problems felt like annoyances. Fatal character flaws became laughable idiosyncrasies. The team became more confident. The opportunities started to pour in. Good begets good.

It's akin to pushing yourself up onto the top of a wall when you haven't been to the gym in months. It's going to take every last bit of strength to get up there, call it survival mode, but once you are there, you can see for miles. You have to believe so much in the possibility of what could be that you must completely tune out what's wrong. Until you can actually address it, which is much later.

Now it's not to say you can't listen. Almost everyone who comes into a leadership role does a listening tour, and they often encounter some degree of simmering employee grievances, personal agendas and sometimes enough political maneuvering to make their head spin. For the sake of the point I am making, I'm deliberately ignoring the positives that come out of these listening sessions, which are also abundant, because I believe by their very nature a listening tour poses a more grave threat to achieving a meaningful vision if not mindfully executed with a vision in mind. What can't be ignored however, are cases of racism, inequity, microaggressions, toxicity, bullying, dishonesty or otherwise serious issues. Those, my friends, need to be fixed. And fast.

Listening tours are important. I usually take notes. I listen. I hear people out. I empathize. Employees might have been in positions where they haven't had an outlet, a career growth path or felt empowered to change the environment around them. They've been focusing on the problems, not the vision, because in many cases, there has been no vision. And most likely, that's why you were hired to lead this particular organization.

CHAPTER 11   CREATE CONNECTIONS: A LITTLE HELP FROM MY FRIENDS

These sessions unlock bottled up experiences which are often intricate in nature. Beware of intricacy. It's a trap door. Intricacy can take you away from setting a bigger vision and acting on that. I've often walked out of some of those first 1:1s feeling like it would take up all my time to fix a single beleaguered employee's reality. But to be honest, I put that on ice. I focus on the one thing that I do have some semblance of ability in: **doing the best work I can with what I have in front of me.**

Here's the reality that most people don't want to accept, you simply have to **make do with what you have** when you come into an organization: the people, the processes, the team structure, the personalities, the culture. It's there and it's not going to change anytime soon. But what you have to summon is the inner strength to do something great with what you have.

You need to dig deep into what you can actually bring to the table: your creative vision, your attention to detail, your ability to encourage the team, your ability to inspire people, your ability to affect even the smallest of things and make it better. You have to leave nothing on the stage.

Focus on what's in front of you. There will never be a perfect project, a perfect brief, the perfect processes in place or a perfect career path laid out in front of you like the yellow brick road. You simply have to make the best you can with what's in front of you. Make that unloved B2B brief something you're proud of. Make that website landing page better than anyone ever thought possible. Make that CEO keynote sparkle. Make the unsexy, unloved work better first. And in doing so you'll solve a lot of problems that no one wanted to solve.

When you step into a new role, it doesn't matter if you were the biggest rockstar in your previous role or at your previous company, you are starting from zero. You may have a little wind in your sails from your reputation or the endorsement by your new manager, but you need to build a whole new

CHAPTER 11 CREATE CONNECTIONS: A LITTLE HELP FROM MY FRIENDS

credibility from the ground up. This is a new team, a new challenge and it's up to you. You must deliver first and make the changes later. **After you show what YOU can do with what you have.**

And guess what, whoever hired you started the clock the minute you started. No one likes to say that out loud because it sounds rather harsh, but you're in a race against time to demonstrate value to the organization. You have to prioritize like your life depends on it, because your livelihood does.

This prioritization is what trips people up. Instead of focusing on what they can actually bring to the table, they focus on getting the table setting just right. You have to get to the table and show everyone what you can do or you'll never get the fine china. Over and over, those who focus most of their time on "what could be" always lap the people that focus on what elements need to change, what leadership could be doing differently or who on the team could be doing something differently. Often they are the most deeply insecure employees who are the most fearful of actually putting their own ability on full display and exerting actual effort to fix the broken things. And in turn, because their focus is on the wrong things, they drive the least impact for the business.

It requires much less effort to "point and punish" than it does to dive in and make something better so some employees sink into these behaviors. It's important to identify and make a note of the armchair critics and make sure to monitor the balance of complaining vs. impact.

On every given day, there are a litany of things that are disappointing, foreboding or challenging. It's the ability to be "eyes on the prize" and constantly push your brain to get out of the complaint swamp and look at the horizon line that separates those who rise to the middle and those that rise to the top.

CHAPTER 11   CREATE CONNECTIONS: A LITTLE HELP FROM MY FRIENDS

I've heard leaders say things like, "I was not set up for success," when they talk about leaving a job, getting fired or not being promoted. This problematic phrase implies everyone else around you is responsible for your success, so much in fact that whoever hired you is solely responsible for setting you up. And let me tell you, they have other things to do. Beyond the cursory onboarding, goal setting, guidance and advice you may receive from a manager, the rest of the setting up for success falls on you.

You are actually the only person who can set you up for success. By understanding the business, by reading the research, by forming the relationships, by understanding the organizational dynamics, by learning the culture, by creating the inroads. And most importantly, by delivering great work with whatever tools, experience and strategies you bring.

As a way to help me focus on the goals, I often visualize swimming to an island that's far in the distance. Under the surface looms a dark underbelly of eels and long tendrils of seaweed that will wrap around my legs and pull me down unless I keep moving and keep paddling on the surface, staying horizontal. These things creep up all the time. It might be a toxic individual, a rabbit hole of distraction, a loosely held negative opinion, a company fear, the list goes on. Usually these things drift away once good work is in place.

In my career, I've been most heavily praised for my ability to get great work out of a previously dismissed, disparaged or denounced team, brand, client, agency, company or individual. And I have to say, it's been the most gratifying work to turn something around. To change perception, blow through benchmarks and to watch people discover what's been in them all along.

Throughout my career, my strategy has been simple. Focus on possibility. And ignore the rest.

As a leader, you must not get pulled down into the swamp of minutiae and complaints. Don't let the tendrils of personal agendas, politics and process problems wrap around your legs and pull you below the surface.

CHAPTER 11   CREATE CONNECTIONS: A LITTLE HELP FROM MY FRIENDS

Don't wait for the perfect glassy water and perfect sunlight to dive in. As a leader, you were most likely hired because it's gray skies, choppy water and lots and lots of seaweed on the bottom.

You might be breathless and scared. You might be looking at the long stretch between where you are and dry land. But remember, there are people swimming beside you. That's your team. You must remind them all the time about the beautiful island that all of you are headed towards. And once you are swimming together, their energy and vision will carry you too.

No matter what you must keep swimming forward. Quickly. Remember, the clock started the minute you dove in.

Every time you feel those cunning coils from the bottom try to pull you down, sweep them away as quickly as possible. Teach your team to look ahead and focus on the island. You must make sure they don't get pulled down either. That is your job as a leader.

Xanthe Wells
VP Global Creative, Pinterest

***

Care. Care about people. Care about who they are. Who they want to be. Care about their growth. Care about their next job. Care about improving their weaknesses. Care about navigating their fears. Care about how they might receive your message. Or your behavior. Care about how you prop them up with praise. Care about how you share the difficult stuff. Care enough to be fully present to whoever is in front of you. Care to take a moment for a smile, a joke, a story or a hug. Care even when they don't. Care. They will not just see it and hear it and know it. They will feel it. And that will make all the difference.

Paul Venables
Founder, Chairman, Venables Bell + Partners

CHAPTER 12

Create Understanding: Final Exam

I did mention that there would be a test at the end. No surprises. But don't worry, you already have the answers. Here goes:

How did I do?

Do you feel like I set you up for success? Did I explain my opinions? Did I overexplain them? Was I open to opinions besides my own? Did I deliver on my promises? Was I helpful? Did I walk the talk? Even though we've never met, do you feel like you've gotten to know me? Could we spend a few hours in an airport lounge together? Do you feel like you can trust me? Would you come to me with tough problems and to give me honest feedback? Do you think I would listen? Would you want to work on my team? Was I grateful for the time you spent reading this book? Did I make you feel something?

I hope the answer is yes. Because that means this stuff works.

CHAPTER 13

Create Gratitude (Part 3): Thank You

I mean it.

Acknowledgments

Thank you to my wife for giving me space to write and laughing at my jokes. To my daughter who is always honest with her feedback. My parents for supporting my creativity, and not freaking out when I said I wasn't going to med school. Naomi Ramsden for her legal advice and Tony Ramsden for his scout's honor. My teams at Apple and LinkedIn for helping me grow into the leader I am. Simon Pickford for setting me on the path to leadership. Andrew DeBenedictis for ordering the melon, Anastacia Maggioncalda for enabling me to be the CEO of my team, and Tavia Holmes who always leads with her heart.

Thank you to the team at Apress for supporting my writing style. Thank you Matt Hofherr for planting the idea in my head that I should write a book in the first place. Tyler Wilson for giving me the gift of Rick Rubin's *The Creative Act*. Dany Lennon for her insight and advice. Randy Roberts and Wendy Wallbridge for coaching me to be a better leader. Paul Venables for literally and figuratively opening the door.

Thank you to my friends who helped out in the Help From My Friends section. Thank you to my fellow authors Cameron Day, Thomas Kemeny, Dan Nelken, PJ Pereira, Jason Sperling, Jason Harris, Wendy Keller, Rusty Shelton, Kurt Schmidt, Nick Cohen, and Lissa Soep for their guidance on how to approach this whole crazy process. And thank you Luke Sullivan who has always returned my letters/calls/emails ever since I sent him my first portfolio in the mid 90's.

Thanks to everyone who I forgot to thank, and for not holding that against me. Thanks in advance to everyone who says nice things about this book or otherwise promotes it. Oh, is that exit music I hear playing? Okay, Thank you all.

Index

A
Action bias, 34, 35, 101
Apple, 3, 66, 80–83, 116, 131, 132, 179, 180, 208, 209
    culture, 50–53, 81
    and LinkedIn, 53, 80
    scalability, 126
Apple Stores, 124, 125
Asai, Hiroki, 191

B
Bagley, Jason, 206
Batthany, Jean, 188
Biases, 34, 100–101

C
Chang, Emily, 200
Clarity, 15–17, 53, 202
Collins, Brian, 186
Conversations
    with co-workers, 39
    with clients, 39, 144, 152
    with direct reports, 9, 25, 28, 37, 46
    easy conversations, 39
    tough conversations, 39, 40

Creative direction, 8, 53, 107, 110, 198
Creative vision/personal brand
    definition, 166
    get/feel/believe, 175–177
    management and leadership, 180
    narratives, 170–174
    opportunities, 164
    personality, 177–179
    rebrands, 167
    relationship to brand, 167
    storytelling, 170–175
    truth-telling, 168
Cultural values, 51, 52, 55, 64, 65, 76–77
Culture
    agency culture, 8, 36, 56, 57, 60, 72
    at Apple, 50–53, 81
    breaks, 62
    build friendships, 69–70
    build gratitude, 75–76
    company culture, 50, 61, 67–68
    creativity, 56–57, 61
    extracurricular creativity, 63
    failure, 67–68
    fun creative, 70

INDEX

Culture (*cont.*)
    hard work, 61
    honesty, 66–67
    at LinkedIn, 52–55
    mentorship, 60–61
    openness, 73–74
    opportunities, 65–66
    overcommunication, 58–60
    persistence, 64
    relationships, 57–58
    share credit, 64
    storytelling, 75

D

Davis-Lyons, Oriel, 198
Diversity, 98–101, 164, 187, 194, 210
Duncan, Amani, 196

E

Edwards, Geoff, 184
Ewing, Cameron, 208

F

Feedback
    agency's brand, 119–120
    ask questions, 112–113
    brands, 115–119
    brief, 120–121
    clients, 129–131
    consistency, 137–138
    consumer, 121–124
    context, 124–125
    creative review, 136, 137
    decision process, 135
    direction, 109, 110
    empathy, 111
    execution, 128–129
    overcommunication, 114
    praise, 111–112
    presentation, 126–128
    scalability, 125–126
    subjectivity, 133
Functional skills, 15, 45, 160

G

Gallop, Cindy, 197
Gratitude, 1, 77, 157–161, 223

H

Hahn, Greg, 189
Holmes, Tavia, 207
Honest feedback, 43, 67, 69, 221

I

iPod, 127

J

Johnson, Margaret, 184

K

Knight, Linda, 190
Koppel, Adam, 199

L

Lennon, Dany, 213
Lesser, Jim, 204
LinkedIn, 180
   and Apple, 53, 80
   brand guidelines, 118
   collaboration, 53–54
   culture, 52–55, 65
   mentorship, 60
   team building, 80–81
Lynch, Kevin, 201

M

Mizrahi, Isaac, 201
Morgan, Adam, 207

N

Nike, 88, 115, 116

O

One-to-ones
   brainstorm solutions, 29–31
   easy conversations, 39
   format, 20
   goals, 26–27, 29
   going off-script, 33
   interview, 94–96
   managing up, 44
   one-to-many, 40–42
   problem solving, 30, 35–38
   promises, 25
   regularly scheduled time, 20
   relationships with clients, 42–44
   scripts, 22–25, 28, 46–47
   skill development, 27
   tough conversations, 39–40
   venting vs. problem
      solving, 33–34
   virtuous cycle, 32–33
Overcommunication, 4, 36, 58–60,
   77, 114, 178

P

Panel interview, 96–97, 101
Pereira, P.J., 184
Personal brand, *see* Creative
      vision/personal brand
Positive feedback, 19, 39
Positive reinforcement,
   157–159, 161
Presentation skills, 26, 27, 30
Problem solving, 30, 34–38, 207

Q

Quaker Oats Company, 117, 118

R

Relationships
   with clients, 8, 43, 57, 82, 83,
      130, 144, 145, 186, 205

Relationships (*cont.*)
   with co-workers, 57, 178
   with direct reports, 28, 46
Repetition, 15, 21, 25, 46, 59
Rizuto, Rafael, 193
Roan, Tim, 212
Robinson, Jaime, 194
Roe, Kelly, 203

S

Scalability, 13, 82, 125–126
SC Johnson, 116, 117
Selling work
   brand as cool, 147, 148
   client feedback, 148–153
   last time/this time/next time
      paradigm, 146, 147
   one-to-ones, 143
   practice, 145–146
   presentation, 144
   reinforce culture, 144
   tradeoffs, 154
Skinner, B.F., 157, 158, 161
Skinner Box, 158
Skip levels, 45
Sperling, Jason, 213
Sullivan, Luke, 197

T

Talent portfolio, 87–94
Team building
   biases, 100–101
   CEO of your team, 79–80
   create organizational
      system, 80–86
   diversity, 98–101
   external agencies, 85
   firing people, 102–103
   hiring process
      involvement, 104–105
   interview team, 96–98
   models, 84–85
   offer, 102
   one-to-one interview, 94–96
   panel interview, 96–97, 101
   talent portfolio, 87–94
   thank you notes, 101
Transparency, 3, 4, 11, 12, 96, 202

U

Unconscious biases, 100, 101
User experience, 112, 123, 147

V

Venables, Paul, 219
Visionaries, 163–164

W, X, Y, Z

Wei, Dean, 210
Wells, Xanthe, 219
Wieden+Kennedy, 153, 157, 168, 172, 208

GPSR Compliance

The European Union's (EU) General Product Safety Regulation (GPSR) is a set of rules that requires consumer products to be safe and our obligations to ensure this.

If you have any concerns about our products, you can contact us on

ProductSafety@springernature.com

In case Publisher is established outside the EU, the EU authorized representative is:

Springer Nature Customer Service Center GmbH
Europaplatz 3
69115 Heidelberg, Germany